JOURNEY THROUGH ACTS

PART I

The Awakening Apostles

Albert P. Stauderman

C.S.S. Publishing Co.
Lima, Ohio

JOURNEY THROUGH ACTS Book 1

LIBRARY OF CONGRESS
Library of Congress Cataloging-in-Publication Data

Stauderman, Al.
    Journey through Acts.

    Contents: pt. 1. The awakening Apostles.
    1. Bible. N.T. Acts—Criticism, interpretation, etc.
I. Title.
BS2625.2.S7   1989   226'.607   88-24050
    ISBN 1-55673-111-6 (pt. 1)

9822 / ISBN 1-55673-111-6   PRINTED IN U.S.A.

Table of Contents

Part I — *The Awakening Apostles*
(The present volume)

Part II — *The Road to Rome*
(A companion volume)

A Note to the Reader

Supporting passages from *The Acts of the Apostles* are indicated at the beginning of most chapters. By reading the biblical passages, you will complete the reading of the entire *Book of Acts*. Biblical quotations in this book are from the Revised Standard Version of the Holy Bible, but any translation can helpfully be used for purposes of comparison and for additional insights.

Author's Preface

This book has been written to help you share the excitement and the high sense of mission that prevailed during the first thirty years of Christian history. It deals with events recorded in the biblical book we know as *The Acts of the Apostles*.

For reasons of convenience (and cost), *Journey Through Acts* is being published in two volumes. This first book deals with the period from the Ascension of Jesus to the conversion of Saul. The second volume deals chiefly with the adventures of Paul and his companions on "The Road to Rome" and will appear under that title.

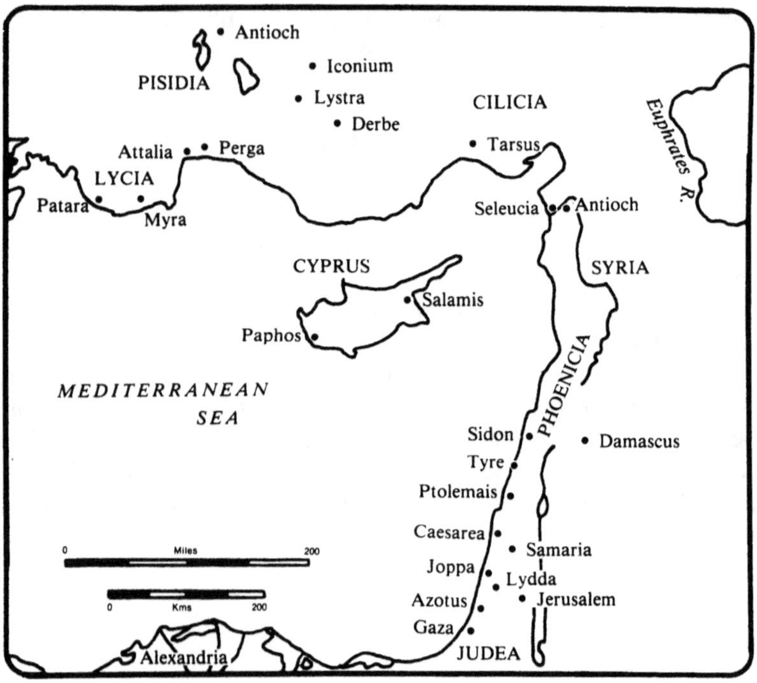
Antioch
Iconium
PISIDIA
Lystra
CILICIA
Derbe
Euphrates R.
Attalia
Perga
Tarsus
LYCIA
Patara
Myra
Seleucia
Antioch
CYPRUS
SYRIA
Salamis
Paphos
PHOENICIA
MEDITERRANEAN
SEA
Sidon
Damascus
Tyre
Ptolemais
Caesarea
Samaria
0 Miles 200
Joppa
Lydda
Azotus
Jerusalem
0 Kms 200
Gaza
Alexandria
JUDEA

Introducing Acts

If you enjoy reading newspapers or magazines, you will like the Book of *Acts*. It's a journalist's account of some events during the first century of the Christian era, events that involved intimate friends of Jesus. It opens with the departure of Jesus from earth, some forty days after the Resurrection, and carries the story forward until the time when the Gospel was being freely preached and taught at Rome, the metropolis of the world. While there are other historical books in the Bible, *Acts* is unique, for it was written by a reporter as a news story.

The writer was a good journalist. Like any good journalist, he drew on many sources. He interviewed people, he consulted documents, he verified facts by talking with a variety of witnesses, he took careful notes and he kept a travel diary. From this store of information, he compiled a coherent and colorful narrative.

Like many important news stories, *Acts* does not have a byline. Other books in the Bible identify their author. In Paul's epistles, for example, he usually places his name at the top of the letter so there's no doubt about the authorship. But to discover the identity of the author of *Acts*, we have to look for hidden clues.

The first indication comes in the very first verse, where the writer addresses someone named Theophilus and refers to an earlier book in which he had dealt "with all that Jesus began to do and teach." Already then we have learned something about the author: he had written a previous book, a book that dealt with the life of Jesus.

If we compare the beginning of the *Gospel According to Saint Luke* with this introductory verse of *Acts*, we will find further information.

Inasmuch as many have undertaken to compile a narrative of the things which have been accomplished among us, just as they were delivered to us by those who were eyewitnesses and ministers of the word, it seemed good to me also, having followed all things closely for some time past, to write an orderly account to you, most excellent Theophilus, that you may know the truth concerning the things of which you have been informed. (Luke 1:1)

Comparing the beginning of these two books gives us a treasurehouse of clues. Both books are addressed to Theophilus, to whom in one case the adjective "most excellent" is applied. Theophilus is a Greek name meaning "lover of God." Some authorities think that both books were written for a Christian community which called itself "Lovers of God," but more likely Theophilus was a Roman official, for they were usually designated as "most excellent," or at least he was a rich and prominent individual. The fact that both Luke and Acts are addressed to the same person or group seems sufficient evidence to assure us that the writer of both books is the same person.

However, we learn much more about Luke from the verse quoted above. He is one of the many writers of biographies of Jesus. We have grown accustomed to thinking of the four Gospels which are included in our Bibles as the only authoritative references for the life of Christ, but in the early church there were many people who compiled some kind of narrative about the life and works of Jesus.

Of the four who wrote the Gospels which have endured to become part of the canon of our Bible, two were among the original disciples. Matthew and John traveled with Jesus, listened to him teach, witnessed the events of his last days. For three years they woke and slept, ate and drank, walked and taught with him.

Mark, the writer of what is believed to be the earliest of the Gospels, was not one of the Twelve. I have always liked to believe that he was a teenager who followed along with the disciples. One reason for this belief is that on the night when Jesus was betrayed, following after the disciples was a young man who was wearing only a linen cloth, perhaps a nightshirt. When the soldiers who arrested Jesus tried to seize this young man, he slipped out of his flimsy garment and ran away naked. The only place this incident is recorded is in the Gospel of Mark, probably because it was a noteworthy and unforgettable incident in Mark's life. Mark is generally believed to have been a young man whose mother was a devoted Christian and who therefore was permitted to travel with the disciples, perhaps serving them in various ways. Mark's youthfulness is borne out in later events since he accompanied Peter and Paul on some of their journeys and they seemed to look upon him as still a young person.

We therefore can account for the Gospels by Matthew and John, both numbered among the disciples, and by Mark, who at least was within earshot of Jesus' teaching and was able to observe some of his miraculous activities. And there were also "many" writers whose works unfortunately have not been preserved for us.

Who Was Luke?

But what about Luke? He was a Johnny-come-lately, a person who entered the picture very late. Luke states that he had followed the life of Christ closely "for some time past," but Luke was not an eyewitness. He admits that his writings are based on the testimony of others who were "eyewitnesses and ministers of the word." Luke's Gospel also differs from the others because he wrote in a more grammatical and literary form of Greek, indicating perhaps a better educational background. Furthermore, he addresses his Gospel to a Greek, or at least someone with a Greek name.

Luke was a reporter who used extreme care in establishing the facts. He checked his stories for accuracy. He interviewed in depth some of those who were closest to Jesus. He had some special relationship with Mary, the mother of Jesus, for only in Luke's writings do we find intimate revelations about Mary's pregnancy.

In some of Paul's epistles we find references to Luke, as well as to Mark. Both these men were together with Paul on missionary trips where they could have exchanged information and discussed the teaching of Jesus. While in Jerusalem, Luke lodged with Mnason, "an early disciple." (Acts 21:16) At Caesarea, Luke stayed with Philip the Evangelist, one of the seven elders, for two years while Paul was awaiting trial. (24:27) All these were opportunities to obtain information from original sources and would have appealed to an eager reporter who was striving to weave all the threads of his story together. Looking ahead a little farther, we will find that Luke was a gentile, the only gentile writer of the New Testament!

While Luke's Gospel was based on the testimony of others, in Acts we find evidence of firsthand reporting. In chapter 16, we can discover some important information from the use of pronouns.

"And *they* went through the region of Phrygia and Galatia . . ." (16:6)

"And when *they* had come opposite Mysia . . ." (7)

". . . passing by Mysia, *they* went down to Troas . . ." (8)

"And a vision appeared to Paul in the night . . ." (9)

"And when he had seen the vision, immediately *we* sought to go on into Macedonia . . ." (10)

"Setting sail . . . *we* made a direct voyage . . ." (10)

Why the sudden change in pronoun from *they* to *we*? The narrative had gone on for fifteen chapters in the third person: "they" did this and that. Then a man from Macedonia comes into the picture and immediately it becomes a first-person story. "We" go on into Macedonia.

The first-person pronoun continues throughout the rest of this chapter of *Acts*. "We remained in the city . . . we supposed there was a place of prayer . . . we sat down and spoke . . . we were met by a slave girl." There is good reason to believe that at this point the narrative becomes the personal account of Luke, the Greek. If this is true, then Luke was the man from Macedonia who appealed to Paul to "come over and help us," or at least he was with the man from Macedonia, who may very well have been Theophilus. At this time the story in *Acts* becomes the personal experience of Luke, who no longer depends on others for eyewitness accounts but who is himself in the midst of the action.

Luke went with Paul across the Aegean Sea to Macedonia, to the major city of Philippi which is well-known to Bible readers because of the epistle later directed by Paul to the Philippians. The group remained at Philippi for some days. When Paul's entourage leaves Philippi, the pronoun reverts to *they*. "They left Macedonia . . . they came to Thessalonica . . . they went into the Jewish synagogue." It therefore seems that Luke remained temporarily in Philippi while Paul and the others went on through Greece, meeting with groups of Christian believers and finally preaching in the great city of Athens.

Many months later, Paul returned to Philippi and once again the narrative switches from the third person to the first. "We sailed away from Philippi . . ." (20:6) in order to go to Jerusalem. Luke was going with Paul on the trip to Jerusalem and was to spend much time with him later, accompanying him on the rest of his missionary journeys.

It seems clear from this evidence that Luke was a Greek, a member of the tiny Christian community in Greece, probably a resident of Philippi. One additional important fact crops up in Paul's letter to the Colossians. Near the end of this little book (Colossians 4:14) Paul writes that "Luke the beloved physician and Demas greet you." If Luke was indeed a Greek physician, he was a scientist of some training and ability. While medicine was far from an exact science in those days, it did require some formal education and an understanding of human nature, which helps explain Luke's compassion and also his concern for detailed information. Luke's accuracy in quoting historical names, places and other facts helps greatly in placing the biblical narrative in its historical perspective.

One more fact about Luke appears in the closing chapter of Paul's second letter to Timothy. Ailing and lonely, Paul awaits death almost eagerly, looking for the "crown of righteousness" which is the reward for those who are faithful to the end. Demas has deserted him; Crescens and Titus have left on other business. "Luke alone is with me. Get Mark and bring him with you, for he is very useful in serving me." (2 Timothy 4:11) So Luke was the sole faithful companion of Paul during those last days.

We have now assembled a lot of facts about Luke. He was a Greek, a gentile, a convert to Christianity who investigated and reported on the life and teaching of Jesus, a companion of Paul on his later missionary journeys. A gifted writer, he produced two lengthy documents for someone named Theophilus. The first we know as the *Gospel According to Saint Luke* and the second we title *The Acts of the Apostles*.

Luke and Mary

Since Luke was a physician, it is interesting to conjecture why and how he became the close confidant of Mary and the only person to recount the intimate details of the conception and birth of Jesus. How did Luke get this information? The first contact Luke had with Mary was in the year A.D. 56, when he came with Paul to Jerusalem to attend the council of the church. One of the members of the host congregation was Mary. She would at that time have been a woman in her late seventies, since she was only seventeen or eighteen at the time of the birth of Jesus. Certainly a woman of that age would welcome the presence in the Christian community of a physician, a healer, a Greek who would have had a better medical education than Judean doctors of that period. In the relationship between doctor and patient, it seems highly credible that Mary revealed to Luke the circumstances surrounding the birth of Jesus. It would have been a natural thing to do, especially since Mary, like the others of her generation, was beginning to worry about what would happen when they died. Would Jesus be forgotten? Would there be some way in which people could remember him? This was a common concern among the disciples and it led to the actual writing of the Gospels. In the first years after the time of Jesus, the events of his life were still fresh in the minds of many disciples. There was a large number of people who had seen him in person. Most of them expected a speedy return of Jesus. It was only some thirty years later that the realization dawned on them that Jesus might not return during their lifetime. It became urgent for them to have some documentary evidence by which to pass along their faith. In Mary's case in particular, she needed some confessor to whom she could reveal the dramatic and miraculous events which had surrounded the birth of her son. Luke was the ideal person — an understanding physician who was also devoted to recording accurately and completely the whole story about Jesus and his followers.

We therefore have a good understanding of the reasons which impelled Luke to undertake the writing of his Gospel, even though he notes that many others had already produced some such writings. He had exclusive personal and confidential information from Mary; he had become intimately acquainted with some of the people who had ministered alongside Jesus; and he represented a Greek constituency of the church which needed the written account in its own language and idiom. He therefore wrote the facts as he had received them and sent them on to Theophilus, emphasizing that his was the true and authentic account of the life of Jesus.

But what about the narrative we know as *Acts*? There was no such impelling reason to produce this work. It's a sort of travel diary or compilation. It's not a complete account of the early church, nor does it make any pretense of being complete. The main characters are Peter and Paul, but they are only two among the many disciples who preached and traveled to spread the Gospel of salvation through Christ. As a matter of fact, the very title we give to this story is misleading. *The Acts of the Apostles* makes it sound as if it were a complete compendium of all that was being said and done, whereas more accurately it could be called, *Some Acts of Some Apostles*. The Greek language has no definite article anyway, so the title could well be translated simply, *Acts of Apostles*.

Why Acts Was Written

To find the reason that motivated Luke in this major project, we need to look into the *Book of Acts* itself. There is a theme that runs through it and that gives concrete reality to the need for such a book, which was written at a time when there was grave concern and even despair about the future of the Christian faith and about its ability to survive the persecutions that came both from Nero and the Romans, and on the other side from the Jewish partisans. In such an era of gloom and crisis, Luke felt a need to emphasize hope and to encourage the weak and scattered Christian congregations. We get some keys to the writer's motives from the text itself:

Acts 6:7 "And the word of God increased, and the number of disciples multiplied greatly . . ."

Acts 9:31 "So the church throughout all Judea and Galilee had peace and was built up; and walking in the fear of the Lord and in the comfort of the Holy Spirit it was multiplied."

Acts 12:24 "But the word of God grew and multiplied."

Acts 16:5 "So the churches were strengthened in faith; and they increased in numbers daily."

Acts 19:20 "So the word of God grew and prevailed mightily."

Acts 28:31 ". . . preaching the kingdom of God and teaching about the Lord Jesus Christ quite openly and unhindered."

In these references we can see Luke's intent. At six widely separated points in the book are these little summaries, showing in ever expanding circles the growth and spread of the faith. The first deals with the growth of the church at Jerusalem; the second with its spread throughout Palestine; then into Syria and what we today call Lebanon; next into Galatia which is far to the west; on into Greece and finally into Rome itself where Paul was permitted to preach and teach without interference even though he was technically a prisoner. In a time of doubt and dejection, Luke wrote to reassure those of wavering faith and to enhearten them by reporting and putting on the record the evidence of growth and triumph.

Even today Christians suffer from nagging doubts about the effectiveness of their preaching and teaching, especially when the worldwide trend seems to be away from standards of love and brotherhood. We feel alone and helpless in the face of overpowering evil until we are reassured that we are part of a great worldwide movement that embraces hundreds of millions who acknowledge Jesus Christ as Lord and Savior. If in our time we need this kind of confirmation, think how much it must have meant to those early Christians who faced ridicule, persecution and even martyrdom. To aid such fearstricken and troubled Christians — and perhaps even to bolster his own faith — Luke compiled a record of the growth and achievement that had been made possible in the early church by the power and presence of God's spirit.

Luke the Historian

Since Luke himself was not a firsthand witness to some of the events in his books, we may conjecture about his sources and the validity of his descriptions. Not to pile proof upon proof, but simply to reinforce my insistence that Luke was a most careful and accurate historian, a brief glance at his Gospel reveals how precise and exact he was. Luke's record of the birth of Jesus is the only one that gives us the date (Luke 2:1, 2) and that relates it to events in the outside world. "In those days a decree went out from Caesar Augustus that all the world should be enrolled." It was this decree that compelled Mary and Joseph to travel from Galilee to Bethlehem, the ancestral city for both of them and the place where they were "registered to vote," to put a modern anachronism into the story.

Caesar Augustus was the Roman Emperor from about 27 B.C. until A.D. 14, according to our method of dating. He was ruler for forty-one years. Then Tiberius Caesar took over, around A.D. 14. The preaching of John the Baptizer (Luke 3:1) took place "in the fifteenth year in the reign of Tiberius Caesar." Luke goes on to identify the other rulers of this period, as if to establish beyond a doubt his accurate placement of historical events. It is delightful for any student to have so accurate a source as Luke. He not only makes statements, but documents them with all needed supporting evidence. Surrounding his account of the biblical narrative is the world scene into which it is placed. Such factual substantiation gives credence and strength to all the things that Luke tells us about Jesus and the early church.

In order to relate the events of Acts to what was going on in the rest of the world, a word about dating is necessary. The period covered in Acts is from approximately A.D. 32 to A.D. 65. According to our modern reckoning, Jesus was born about 4 B.C. While this sounds strange, there is an explanation. The dating of the Christian era was first calculated by a monk named Dionysius Exiguus in the sixth century. He placed the time of the birth of Jesus a few years too late. Since Dionysius was laboring without the computers and calculators that make modern mathematics a more exact science, he came remarkably close to the actual date even if he was off by as much as four years. To look back over six centuries and try to pinpoint exactly when something happened would be difficult today; in the time of Dionysius it was impossible.

Dating ancient history is always difficult. The Jewish system of dating stems from the creation of the world, which they reckon to have taken place in the equivalent of our 3761 B.C. Therefore the Jewish year is 5750 when civil calendars in the western world read A.D. 1989. The Romans dated their years from the founding of the city of Rome, set at 753 B.C. According to the Roman calendar, therefore, Jesus would have been born in the year 749 A.U.C. (*ab urbe conditum*, or from the founding of the city). Early Christians worked under difficult circumstances in their efforts to set proper dates for the life of Christ and for events in his life. The date of Easter was switched around dozens of times before the decision by the Council of Nicaea in A.D. 325, which set it on the Sunday following the first full moon in spring. Even now the Eastern Orthodox churches celebrate Easter on a day different from that observed by the western churches, because they still follow a different calendar. Western churches weren't unanimous in their adoption of the Nicean proposal until the Synod of Whitby in A.D. 664.

Historical research and the science of astronomy now show us that there are more accurate methods of dating the birth of Christ than those available to Dionysius the Monk. For example, we know that King Herod died about 2 B.C., by our calendar. Since Herod was the king who ordered the slaughter of all male infants in Bethlehem who were two years old or younger, this would mean that the birth of Jesus certainly took place before 2 B.C. and probably as early as 4 B.C. Some authorities place his birth at 6 or 7 B.C.

Astronomers have also calculated that there was a notable configuration of heavenly bodies about 5 B.C., when three planets were in conjunction. This might very well have been the signal which alerted the magi to the ancient prophecy about the signs that would accompany the birth of the ruler of the Jews.

While we do not know the exact day or year of the birth of Jesus, thanks to Luke's information we can confidently place it somewhere between 7 B.C. and 4 B.C. on our calendar.

Another factor that helps set the dates for the ministry of Jesus on earth is the coming of John the Baptizer. We owe our knowledge of the time when John came onto the scene to the very accurate historical placing in Luke's Gospel. As noted above, John began preaching in the fifteenth year of the reign of Tiberius Caesar, when Pontius Pilate was governor of Judea and Herod was tetrarch of Galilee, Philip and Lysanias tetrarchs of other regions, and Annas and Caiaphas were the high priests. This assembly of facts gives us at least six points of reference, making it possible to date the start of John's ministry by both the Roman and Jewish calendars.

Tiberius Caesar lived from 42 B.C. to A.D. 37. He was an adopted son of Augustus Caesar, who in A.D. 4 declared him to be his heir. When Augustus died in A.D. 14, Tiberius succeeded him and the "fifteenth year of his reign" would therefore be A.D. 29. However, an earlier decree by Augustus had made Tiberius his equal as a ruler of the Roman provinces. This decree was issued in A.D. 11 or A.D. 13 and as a result historians solemnly debate whether the "fifteenth year" was reckoned in Judea from A.D. 11, 13 or 14.

In any event, this dating of John would set the time of his preaching either at A.D. 27 or 29. Since the active ministry of Jesus spanned three years, this dating of John would indicate that the earthly ministry of Jesus ended when the Crucifixion took place somewhere between A.D. 30 and 32. The Gospel narratives thus cover a period from about 4 B.C. to A.D. 32, a span of thirty-six years.

Taking up the story, the book of *Acts* covers the period from the Ascension, forty days after the resurrection of Jesus, to the closing years of Paul's life when he was preaching and teaching at Rome. This would therefore be from about A.D. 32 to A.D. 63, a span of thirty-one years.

Because Luke's Gospel is a biography, it proceeds chronologically from Jesus' birth to a climax at his death and resurrection. The book of Acts is somewhat different. It is an account of the spread of Christianity and the growth of the church, but it makes no pretense of being a complete and consistent account and simply moves from one incident to another without any great dramatic climax. Yet it shows the Faith starting from the little band at Jerusalem and overcoming obstacles as it spreads to the limits of the Roman world until the message that had first been heard along the dusty roads of Galilee was openly proclaimed in the great world capital of Rome. No persecution could quench it or even cause it to retreat, for the people who followed the way of Jesus were bold in facing death since a better life was awaiting them. By the time of the close of Acts, no single individual or group was indispensable to the church. It could get along

without Peter, or without Paul, because there were Christians everywhere inspired to take up the cause if others laid it down. Martyrdom
like that of Stephen had only stiffened the resolve of others and led
to the conversion of those who admired his courage and steadfast-
ness. Even the lions of the Roman arena and the vicious persecutions of Nero could only cause brief setbacks, for the growth of the
faith continued. That's the story that *Acts* tells.

Chapter 1

The Ascension

Read Acts 1:1-14

There are brief references to the departure or "ascension" of Jesus from earth in the Gospels according to Mark and Luke, although the closing verses of Mark are considered to be a later addition. Matthew tells only of a post-resurrection meeting between Jesus and his disciples on a mountain in Galilee.

Acts provides a somewhat fuller account of the Ascension. While Luke's Gospel says that at the end Jesus blessed the disciples and "parted from them," *Acts* gives us more detail about the leave-taking of Jesus from his disciples on the mount called Olivet, near Jerusalem.

To cover the forty days that separate the Resurrection from the Ascension, *Acts* has only two brief comments. It says that Jesus was with the disciples during this period and "presented himself alive by many proofs." None of these is described further, perhaps because such information is included in the Gospels. The second comment adds the admonition given by Jesus to his followers, directing them to remain in Jerusalem and promising that they will be "baptized with the Holy Spirit."

A Different Kind of Kingdom

When the disciples gathered for their last meeting on earth with their Lord, their major concern was to propound again the familiar question, "Will you restore the kingdom to Israel?" The fact that Jesus had repeatedly warned that his kingdom was not an earthly political organization had not yet sunk in. They were still looking for a military revolution that would free Israel from Roman rule.

What they asked, in effect, was, "Lord, is this the time to throw out those Roman rulers so that we may have our earthly kingdom back again?" The import of Jesus' life, death and resurrection was still hidden from them.

It's always shocking to realize how unperceptive the disciples could be. During the years they had spent with Jesus, they had heard his message dozens of times and had surely discussed it among themselves, but still they seemed to have no comprehension of his real mission. Wouldn't you think that by this time the disciples would have realized that the kingdom Jesus promised was not of this world, that it was a spiritual kingdom? He had stressed this many times. Yet at this crucial final moment the disciples were still at square one. Peter was ready once more to draw his sword and the rest were evidently eager to rouse the populace and start the revolt against Rome. The peaceful patience of Jesus contrasts as usual with the activist and worldly outlook of the impetuous disciples, but he knew that with the coming of Pentecost their eyes would be opened. They would then finally recognize that the real power, the power of the Spirit, is spiritual power.

So patiently and comfortingly, Jesus tried to explain that he was not going to establish or restore an earthly kingdom. As he had done often before, he pointed out that "times and seasons" are in God's hand alone. It was not God's plan to turn to political processes or to set up his rule over the hearts of humanity by some miraculous intervention; God's plan was for the disciples and their converts to do it themselves through the power conferred on them by the Holy Spirit.

"You shall be my witnesses," he said to the disciples. "You shall receive power." He said it would start at Jerusalem, although this was something the disciples were not eager to hear. Jerusalem was the place where Jesus had been mocked and scorned and crucified; Jerusalem was where the disciples had denied Jesus, where they had forsaken him and fled in terror from the high priest's strongarm squad. Everything that frightened and dampened the spirits of the disciples seemed to be related to Jerusalem. They felt safe and at ease in Galilee or in the small towns of Judea, but in the big city of Jerusalem they found it hard to cope. Most of them were fishermen or small-town people who felt out of place among the snobbish and overbearing priests, the brutal soldiers and the materialistic populace of Jerusalam. Yet this was where they were to start their mission!

It has always delighted me that Jesus made this so clear to those apprehensive disciples, for it teaches me something. When you have had a failure, you can't run away and start somewhere else. You have to stand up where you fell down! If a toddler tries to walk across the room but stumbles and falls down, he has to get up right at that same place. So Jesus impresses upon the disciples that Jerusalem, the place where they had become undone, was also the place where they must start to piece things together. Then their witness could be taken out into the friendlier villages of Judea and even into Samaria.

Why did Jesus mention Samaria? Samaria and its people were usually shunned by the Jews. The Samaritans were a mixed race and were looked upon with scorn, even though they worshiped the same God and claimed to share the same heritage as the Jews. They dwelt in the region between Judea and Galilee, an area that had been the battleground between the Northern Kingdom and the Southern Kingdom in the years when Israel was divided. So sending the disciples to witness in this impoverished area was like sending them into the slums. The disciples had traveled through Samaria on their journeys with Jesus and had witnessed with some disdain his willingness to meet with and teach these people. Now the area was placed on their agenda for witnessing as they spread out to the "end of the earth."

One must wonder how much of this parting message from Jesus really registered with the disciples. They would have preferred to return to their home towns, to the quiet surroundings of Galilee, there to await the glory that they hoped would come. Instead, they were being told to take to the road and go into strange and unknown places. As far as we know, none of the disciples had ever been far from home. Hitherto their activities had been confined to a narrow and circumscribed area about 150 miles long and fifty miles wide. How could they even picture the "ends of the earth"? Not until Pentecost did the possibility seem real to them of witnessing and preaching and teaching in faraway places where there were different languages, different people and an alien mode of life.

Jesus' Departure

The narrative then takes us on to the actual ascension event. Unfortunately, our impression of this happening has been shaped by the works of medieval artists whose paintings often depicted Jesus levitated above the gaping disciples, his bare feet dangling a yard or so over their heads. Many stained-glass church windows have imprinted this version on the minds of receptive worshipers. I remember especially one church in Trenton, New Jersey, where a huge chancel window portrays this scene on a heroic scale. It shows Jesus, his arms flapping as though in flight, with his bare toes just above the heads of the disciples as they stare upward in wonder. That's the sort of picture that has influenced the beliefs of many people about this event. We allow artists and editorial writers and commentators to make up our minds for us when we ought to make them up ourselves, based on our understanding of the facts.

But how can anyone depict the Ascension? If a cloud hid Jesus from sight, as Luke states, what's an artist going to do for a picture? There has to be some way of showing what presumably happened. That's what artists have tried to do, but their interpretation lingers in our minds rather than the more rational description given by Luke.

Translating spiritual things into visible images distorts them. Some years ago, Roark Bradford wrote the stories which Marc Connelly later wove into the great play, *Green Pastures*. The play included a scene in which a group of little children in a Sunday school class were listening while the teacher tried to describe to them what God was like. The best example the teacher could give was the venerable preacher in the next town, a stout black man with a dignified manner and a gray beard. "God looks like that preacher," the teacher said as an image formed in the minds of the children. Or we have seen great paintings like Michelangelo's in the Sistine Chapel in Rome, depicting God as a large gray-bearded individual whose hand is reaching out to give life to Adam. Such things may give us a mental handle to grasp things that can never be adequately depicted, but they warp our views, even though it may be unconsciously and unintentionally.

Luke describes the Ascension by saying simply, "He was lifted up." That is a term occurring frequently in the Scriptures. Jesus said of his crucifixion, "If I be lifted up, I will draw all men to me." The phrase is used similarly in other places and appears to mean to be brought closer to God.

Luke's writing naturally had to use terms which had meaning to those who read it. If the writing was to make sense to them, it had to be phrased in ways they could comprehend. The idea of "ascension" was therefore in keeping with the general conception of the universe in those times. To the ancients, the cosmos had three levels. Somewhere below the earth was the pit, the lower level, the abode of Satan and the place of the damned, the underworld. Human beings lived on the middle level, the earth. Somewhere up above was the place where the gods lived. The Greeks — of whom Luke was one — pictured their gods to be living atop a high mountain. So heaven, the abode of God, was thought of as being high above the earth.

Heaven may or may not be a place, but if it is a place it is so much beyond my conception that I cannot begin to describe it. Bible writers could describe it only by using the richest and most glowing concepts — gates of pearl, streets of gold. Today we know that the physical universe is beyond comprehension, and ideas like "God" or "heaven" are greater than anything we can imagine or describe. Heaven is probably best defined, if indeed it must be defined at all, as a state of joy and blessedness where God's love rules and where sin, evil and mortality are unknown. It is the place or the state of being where God's will is done without interference, for we pray in the words of Jesus that his will "be done on earth as it is in heaven."

This may not mean that there cannot be something comparable to material things in heaven. Perhaps the souls of the redeemed who enjoy heavenly bliss can recognize one another and perhaps they can even engage in useful occupations. The Swedish mystic Emanuel Swedenborg developed a unique conception of heaven. His doctrine was that in heaven you do whatever you liked most to do on earth. If you are an ardent bridge player, you'll find a permanent bridge game going on in heaven. If you're a carpenter, you'll have the best tools to work with. Whatever useful work you like best, providing it is not contrary to God's will, is what you'll do in heaven. And if what you like to do is contrary to God's will, probably you won't get there anyway.

So Luke wisely avoids getting involved in philosophical speculations and tells us plainly and clearly that while the disciples were looking on, Jesus was lifted up and a cloud hid him from their sight. He was suddenly gone. To add anything to this account is mere conjecture and artistic license.

Two Men in White

We can imagine the reaction of the disciples when Jesus was abruptly removed from their midst. They were astonished and they must have looked around in consternation, asking one another, "Where did he go? What happened?"

The answer came from two men in white robes who stood near the stunned disciples. Here again we suffer from the heritage of the artists, who usually depict angels as lovely young women with wings or as chubby youngsters. The Bible gives a different picture. Obviously artists prefer to paint young women or children rather than ordinary men, but when angels appear in the New Testament that's what they are. The angel who greeted the early-arriving women at the tomb on Easter morning was a young man dressed in white. The messenger who announced the birth of Jesus to Mary was named Gabriel. In the Old Testament, one angel was even a prototype of an olympic wrestler, for he struggled all night with Jacob at the brook Jabbok and even threw Jacob's hip out of joint. That was a pretty powerful angel!

Here again, two men were the angels — the messengers of God — who summoned the disciples back to reality. "Why do you stand looking into heaven?" they demanded.

When God sends his messengers, there's no argument. Shocked, confused and distressed, the disciples returned from Olivet to Jerusalem, about a "sabbath day's journey" or a little more than half a mile. They went back to the same upper room that had been their hiding place for forty days and "devoted themselves to prayer," in anxious anticipation of whatever God had planned for them to do next.

Thoughts

(for personal reflection and group discussion)

1. "Parting is such sweet sorrow," according to Shakespeare. Some people hate goodbyes. Others keep saying them over and over again. How did the disciples rate in their leave-taking from Jesus? What might they have done differently?

2. Even to the end, some of the disciples kept hoping that Jesus would establish a worldly power. They evidently could not comprehend a spiritual kingdom. How different have we become?

3. Everyone has a personal concept of heaven, often related to some loved parent or other relative who has died and who seems to deserve happiness after suffering in this life. How would you describe heaven?

Questions

1. When did the Ascension take place? Is "ascension" a proper term to describe the event?

2. How many witnesses were present?

3. What message was given to the disciples?

4. Who were the "men in the white robes" and why did the disciples not talk with them?

5. When the disciples returned to the upper room, how did they react to what they had seen?

Chapter 2

On the Eve of Pentecost

Beset as we are by television, radio, magazines and newspapers, it is hard for us to imagine a society without formal means for disseminating information. In the time of the disciples, however, news was scarce and was often months or even years late. Women who gathered at the well to draw water, or those who spent the morning at the riverside washing clothes, would quite naturally tend to spend their time discussing the events in the community. Another place where information was exchanged is revealed in an ancient Babylonian tablet that reads, "Strife you find among servants, gossip among barbers."

For information about distant places, travelers were the chief source. When a stranger arrived in a village, the first question from the innkeeper or the host would be, "What news do you bring?"

As we know from the parlor game called "Gossip," news transmitted by word of mouth is often subject to great distortion. Sometimes items were exaggerated on purpose. Hoping to be well-received, a guest would often embroider the stories he told about the people and events in the major centers of politics and business.

Some things were written. An important source of information about those times are clay tablets on which business transactions were recorded by ancient scribes. Merchants and tradespeople would engage the services of secretaries or scribes, who often maintained an outdoor "office" near the city gates. They were available for employment when required to write letters or other important documents. By New Testament times, wooden tablets like slates were used and reused for such letters and messages. Also in use was papyrus, a form of paper made from reeds and imported from Egypt. The first Christian writings were on such papyrus scrolls.

In view of the difficulties in communication, it's miraculous that the New Testament books have come down to us as complete as they are. There is no indication that anyone wrote down the words and deeds of Jesus as he proceeded through his ministry, but within a generation his followers realized the importance of preserving them so they inscribed them on the clumsy and expensive writing materials of the time. Perhaps the history of those days would be more complete if the newsgathering facilities of a major newspaper or television network had been at hand, but who knows? Yet it is fun to conjecture. For instance, if the Jerusalem *Post* had been publishing in the year A.D. 33, the following column might well have appeared on the day before Pentecost.

From the column "Jerusalem Merry-Go-Round" by Jacob ben Anders in the *Jerusalem Post*

One of the best-kept secrets around Pilate's palace these days is the whereabouts of a political prisoner who was supposed to have been executed on Passover Eve. The man is said to have been seen in various parts of the city and even in Galilee. He is (or was) a Nazarene prophet who incurred the anger of the High Priest and of the Sanhedrin because of his anti-establishment speeches. He was known as Jesus of Nazareth and was called "rabbi," although he had no formal rabbinical training.

Palace records show that the Nazarene was given a public hearing just before Passover by Governor Pilate at the demand of the High Priest. The Sanhedrin had already considered his case and had recommended that he be put to death on charges of blasphemy. They therefore sent the case on to Pilate, asking for a Roman crucifixion on the charge that the Nazarene wanted to overthrow Caesar. Pilate found no evidence to back up this accusation and refused to issue a judgment. Terming it an internal doctrinal matter affecting only the Jewish religion, Pilate sent the accused man to King Herod, who happened to be in the city at that time. Herod denied that he had jurisdiction in the case, because the alleged crimes took place in Jerusalem. Herod and Pilate have had frequent disagreements since the Romans limited Herod's sphere of authority to Galilee and other northern regions.

Several influential Sanhedrin members including Joseph of Arimathea and Nicodemus disagreed with the conviction of Jesus. They urged Governor Pilate to halt the execution. Palace sources hint that Lady Procula also pleaded with her husband to intervene, but he apparently refused. Pilate reportedly turned the execution over to the Jews, but Jewish law provides for stoning as the means of death. By permitting Jesus to be crucified, Pilate gave the impression that the punishment was being inflicted under Roman law.

An added peculiarity came when palace guards placed a sign on the cross of Jesus which read, "The King of the Jews." They told witnesses that Pilate had ordered the sign placed there. Temple authorities were angered by the sign, considering it in poor taste. They demanded its removal, but Pilate refused their request.

According to Levite authorities, any seizure or punishment of members of ruling families of Israel is prohibited by the occupation agreement. Under this pact, any member of the royal family would have been free from prosecution. The Nazarene, however, was not closely related to the Herodians. He did, according to some records, claim to be a descendant of King David.

This column has learned from sources close to the palace guard that the condemned man actually died on the cross. Death was attested by the centurion in charge and the body was later claimed by Joseph of Arimathea and was secretly taken out of the city.

That would have been the end of the affair except for rumors that have been surfacing throughout Jerusalem in recent weeks. Some disciples of the Nazarene claim that they have met and talked with him since the Passover. One report states that he spoke to a crowd of more than 500 of his followers on a hillside near Jerusalem last month. Several reliable informants have stated to this writer that they saw and spoke with a man who claimed to be the same Jesus as the one who was crucified on Calvary.

When Jesus was teaching in this city and in other parts of the country, he had a cabinet or inner circle of about a dozen followers, mostly Galileans. Some of these returned to their homes after his death, but have since disappeared or gone into hiding. Threats of death by stoning have been made against them if they persist in spreading the dangerous teachings which Jesus originated.

The Jesus affair has stirred administrative circles here in Jerusalem because of its political implications. If the man is not really dead, the military leaders who were to have carried out the crucifixion are in danger of severe punishment. They can be stripped of rank and sentenced to a life term on the galleys. Pilate's secretary says no such action is contemplated. The governor is satisfied that the centurion in charge carried out his duties efficiently.

Another complication deals with the "King of the Jews" sign. Under the occupation pact, Pilate could face recall or demotion if he knowingly permitted personal injury to any member of the Jewish royal family. He has many critics who would eagerly report him to Caesar in Rome.

Since Jesus was not a member of the ruling family, Pilate's actions in placing the sign on the cross must have been intended as a criticism of the Sanhedrin, implying that they did not recognize their own king, or as an insult to the Herodians. In either case, it has caused great indignation among the temple crowd. Oddly enough, King Herod has not joined in the uproar. Relations between him and Pilate have been reported greatly improved in recent weeks.

Four questions remain unanswered. Why did Pilate write that sign? What happened to the body of Jesus? If Jesus really died on the cross, who is the impostor who has convinced so many people that he is Jesus? Or — and this is the most startling question of all — did Jesus somehow survive the crucifixion?

With record crowds expected in the city this week for the Pentecost holiday, both the Sanhedrin and the Roman garrison have taken steps to tighten security so there will be no further incidents like those that marred the Passover. Any followers of Jesus who show up will be kept under close scrutiny.

Thoughts

(for personal reflection or group discussion)

1. The media — newspapers, radio, TV — play such a big role in our lives today that it is hard to imagine getting along without them. Would your life be richer or poorer if there were less radio and TV and fewer magazines and newspapers? Could you do without them entirely?

2. News is often "slanted" and sometimes deliberately distorted. What tests should we apply to the news reports that we see or hear?

3. Our knowledge of the life and teachings of Jesus comes solely from the Gospels. Look back to the first four verses of Luke's Gospel. Do these words encourage you to believe that Luke is a reliable reporter?

Questions

1. How were the words of Jesus preserved for posterity?

2. Were there newspapers in biblical times? If not, how was the news spread through the community?

3. As news of the Resurrection of Jesus spread, what do you suppose were the reactions of Pontius Pilate, King Herod, Roman soldiers, followers of Jesus, ordinary Jewish citizens?

4. Many visitors and pilgrims came to Jerusalem for Pentecost. What story would they take back to their home towns?

5. Why did the disciples remain in hiding during the days between the Ascension of Jesus and Pentecost?

Chapter 3

Pentecost

Read Acts 1:15—2:42

The Jewish feast of Pentecost or *Shavuoth* marked the closing of the spring harvest of grain, which began at the Passover. The observance took place fifty days after the Passover and the Christian church later set it at fifty days after Easter. Pentecost is a Greek word meaning fiftieth.

Because of its climate, Palestine is a two-crop region. Pentecost was the time to offer thanks for the safe gathering-in of the first crop. Then in late September or October came the second thanksgiving for the harvest, called the Festival of Booths or Tabernacles.

The disciples were probably not much disposed to join in any celebration as they watched their countrymen gather in Jerusalem for the Pentecost observance. After the ascension or disappearance of Jesus with its seeming finality, they had retreated to their upper room, confused, bewildered and saddened. It must have seemed like a death in the family. When there is the loss of someone near and dear, the void is great. At such a time people need two things which seem paradoxical — they need the companionship of others in order to share their grief, and they need to be alone with their own thoughts. These two conflicting needs arise whenever there is a great loss.

So the disciples stayed close to one another, sharing their silence and their sorrow. They did not know what was coming next, but they knew that Jesus had been taken away from them and that, whatever came, they would have to face life in a different way. They might never see Jesus again and they had to reconcile the rest of their lives to this new situation.

As they prayed together and took counsel together, they surely remembered things that Jesus had said to them to prepare them for this very event. For one, he had instructed them not to depart from Jerusalem, so they must have made a compact with one another to stay there together as a group. Those were the Master's wishes. And if he should reappear, no one wanted to be in the position of Thomas, who was absent during an earlier appearance of Jesus. So they stayed — and actually stayed for five years. During this time they organized their own religious community or synagogue; they formed a closeknit and somewhat secret cult; they stuck together when they ran into conflicts in encounters with other Jewish sects; and they required protection from time to time by the pagan Romans.

Yet they formed a close brotherhood and sisterhood, supporting one another and trying to be faithful to what Jesus had commanded. During this period there were many occasions when they emerged into public and preached openly and boldly the message that Jesus had entrusted to them, but only to the Jews. It took them at least five years to realize that their message was not confined to a sect within the Jewish faith, but was really intended for the whole world.

Looking for Number Twelve

One of their first acts was to choose a successor to Judas, the betrayer of Jesus, who had come to a bad end and either committed suicide or was stricken with a strange ailment. He died an unpleasant death and this is the end of Judas, so far as the biblical narrative is concerned. He had repented of his betrayal of Jesus, according to Matthew, and threw the thirty pieces of silver that he had received for his treason into the temple, to the dismay of the chief priests and elders. They could not put the money back into their treasury, for it was the "price of blood" and therefore tainted. Matthew says that the priests took the money and bought a plot of ground, "the potter's field," as a place in which to bury strangers. Luke's version is that the money was used by Judas himself, who "bought a field with the reward of his wickedness." In either case, the money was used to buy a field.

Without Judas, only eleven disciples were left. This would not seem to matter much, considering the character of Judas! But twelve is a special number among the Jews, a sacred number which corresponds to the number of the tribes of Israel. Luke's Gospel (22:29) informs us that Jesus had promised the disciples that they would sit on thrones judging the twelve tribes of Israel. They thus felt an urgent need to replace Judas and restore their number to twelve.

Their decision to choose a new apostle is a revelation because Peter takes the lead in the group, acting as a sort of chairman. He directs that the choice must be made from among the men who accompanied the apostles "all the time that the Lord Jesus went in and out among us, beginning from the baptism of John until the day when he was taken from us." Our conventional picture, then, of a band of twelve trudging the roads with Jesus is mistaken. There were others who went the whole way and who were also witnesses of the Resurrection. According to the count given (1:15), about 120 such persons formed the congregation from which the choice was to be made.

They selected two candidates and then prayed and cast lots to select the new apostle. This is the last time in the biblical narrative that such a choice was made by casting lots, perhaps because later choices were guided by the Holy Spirit. We don't know whether they cast dice, or drew straws, or used some other method. Dice, however, are of ancient origin and were frequently used for games by the people of that time. Throughout the Old Testament the use of dice to make a choice was common. Today we would probably take a vote to decide who should be the apostle, but democracy as we know it doesn't fit into the thinking of Bible times. People then believed that to elect a person would be a human choice and not necessarily what God wants. But the casting of lots took the decision out of the hands of humans and the choice was therefore made by a power other than the human mind. It was chance, of course, and we might even call it superstition, but it was not a human choice. Superstitions often work their way into religion, sometimes with a fairly logical basis. Even today we seem to favor seven, twelve or forty, which in ancient times were sacred numbers. And we shun thirteen because that was the number at the table for the last supper just before Jesus' betrayal.

The lot fell to Matthias and he may have joined the others at Pentecost, the day when something happened to the disciples that changed the course of their lives and ours. They were still in the upper room, keeping to themselves, when there was a sound like the rush of a strong wind. Luke's careful and temperate choice of words is clearly evident here. He does not say it was a wind. It was a sound like that of a mighty wind, something inexplicable and yet demanding to be put into words. And resting on each of the apostles was something which "appeared to them tongues as of fire." Again we note that Luke does not say that these were actually blazing flames. Rather, these were the symbols of the Holy Spirit, wind and fire. As Jesus had promised, the power of the Spirit came upon these men in typical fashion, for the Holy Spirit is God at work in the world. A wind exists only when it is blowing. If it is not in action, we say, "There is no wind." A flame exists only when it is burning. So the Holy Spirit is never at rest, never captive, but always in action.

"Other Tongues"

Filled with this Spirit, the apostles "began to speak in other tongues" and rapidly attracted a crowd. It was the reversal of the Tower of Babel, for then people became confused because they could no longer understand one another. Here, people from all parts of the world were amazed because they could perfectly understand what the disciples were saying.

This was not the "speaking in tongues" which some people claim to experience as a result of the Holy Spirit's presence. In the Corinthian church, "speaking in tongues" was an incoherent form of speech, unintelligible to those who heard it. Advocates of tongues or glossolalia today claim that such speaking comes because of the Spirit's indwelling presence, making it necessary to express one's self whether or not others can understand what is said. Paul later acknowledged that this might be a valid Christian experience, but he said that he would rather speak one word that could be understood than a thousand words of gibberish.

It's fair to ask whether the Pentecost experience was really speaking in unknown tongues, which foreigners only presumed to understand, or whether these apostles by some miraculous gift were actually able to speak in a dozen different languages. However, a group of people speaking loudly in twelve different languages would cause such cacaphony that no one would be able to understand anything, like a faulty radio that pulls in several stations at one time.

Yet by some wonderful power, the people who listened were able to say, "How is it that we hear each of us in his own native language?" Perhaps the miracle was in the hearing rather than in the speaking. At any rate, the people who heard were amazed and perplexed, and this is not surprising. "What can this mean?"they asked.

Peter then once again asserts his leadership, delivering a very interesting sermon. He defends the apostles against a charge some hearers must have made: they were not drunk, it's still only nine o'clock in the morning! This is the fulfilment of a prophecy by Joel that God will pour out his spirit and young men shall see visions and old men shall dream dreams and they shall speak out about the wonders of God. Then Peter goes on to describe the great wonder to which they have been witnesses: the life, death and resurrection of Jesus Christ.

One wonders how Luke was able to record so fully a sermon which he did not hear and which he wrote down some thirty years later. In addition to Peter's sermon at Pentecost, Luke recounts for us a sermon some time later when Peter healed a lame man (3:12-26), Peter's sermon before the Sanhedrin (chapter 4), Peter's sermon to the council and also Stephen's long sermon before he was stoned to death (chapter 7). How did Luke get such verbatim accounts that he has passed along to us?

It was quite customary in those days for such sermons to be put together afterward by peoples' recall of what was said. This does not dilute the truth of Scripture. Even in ancient Greece, where there was much greater literacy, many a great oration was later put down in writing as what the orator said he said or what people remembered from what he said. There were no stenographers or tape recorders.

If you think that sort of thing happened only in ancient Greece, note that we now have cable television which carries the daily happenings in the House of Representatives in Washington. I watch it occasionally and find that almost every time a congressman gets up to speak, he starts by saying, "I ask unanimous consent that I may revise and extend my remarks for the Congressional record." What the representative says on the floor of the House isn't important as far as the written record is concerned. After his brief speech, because they are limited to two minutes, he works up a long speech to insert in the Record. Probably he corrects the grammar and includes comments about his constituents so they may get their names put into the Record, too.

The point is that these teachings, sermons and statements that we find in the Bible were actually made, but later reconstructed from memory and from consultation with others who also heard them. They have therefore come down to us, perhaps not in the exact words in which they were delivered, but with the true meaning and spirit of the original. The disciples certainly assisted one another in recalling the things that Jesus said. They were accustomed to relying more on their memories than we do now. If they honestly put together a composite of the things they remembered we are well served, because the result was sure to be reasonably accurate.

A Call to Repentance

After Peter preached, there was quite a commotion. "What shall we do?" the people asked. "Repent and be baptized, every one of you," said Peter.

The question these people asked was the greatest compliment that can be paid to a preacher. If a sermon spurs listeners into action, it's a success. All too often people listen to a sermon like Tennyson's Northern Farmer, who heard the preacher "a-buzzin' over his head. And I thought he said what he ought to have said, and I came away."

Peter inspired something better. His sermon stirred people into action. The record continues to the effect that some 3,000 adherents were added to the Christian community and many of them were baptized.

Once again let us turn to that imaginary newspaper story on the day after Pentecost, to see what an alert reporter might have made out of the events of the day:

From the Jerusalem *Post*
Sivan 6, 3793 (May 21, A.D. 33)

Preaching of Nazarene Disciples Draws Big Crowd to Temple Area
One of the largest crowds of the Pentecost holiday gathered at Solomon's Porch last evening to listen to speeches by a group of Galileans who claim to be followers of Jesus of Nazareth. Jesus was the itinerant preacher who was crucified here about two months ago after a charge of sedition was brought against him by members of the temple staff.

Police estimated that at least 5,000 persons crowded the temple area, but no incidents were reported or arrests made. The disciples had attracted the attention of the holiday crowd by parading through the city streets with flaming torches atop their heads, according to Centurion Quintus, commander of the Roman guard at the temple. The commotion as the crowd hurried to the open spaces adjacent to the temple sounded like a windstorm, he said.

"Our orders are not to interfere with peaceful religious demonstrations," Quintus told this reporter. He admitted that Rabbi Joab of the temple staff had asked that the demonstration be halted because Peter the Fisherman, a leader of the Galileans, charged that the crucifixion of Jesus had been carried out by "lawless men." Quintus refused to interfere, however, because no disturbance resulted from this charge. He said the crucifixion had been correctly executed by court order and under Roman law.

"I was surprised to hear the speakers talking to the crowd in Latin," Quintus added. "I don't suppose many understood what was being said. I wanted to move in closer so I could hear more clearly what they were saying, but I was afraid the crowd might think I was going to halt the demonstration. This could have led to anti-Roman rioting and Governor Pilate has instructed us to avoid this."

The centurion was mistaken about the language used by the speakers, according to another witness. Montanus of Galatia, a journalist who was visiting here to observe the Pentecost celebrations, said he heard the disciples clearly and that they were speaking in the ancient Phrygian tongue.

"Believe me, I was surprised that there were so many people in Jerusalem who could understand our language so well," he said. "I've had endless trouble trying to converse with people in this city."

Several local people who were in the crowd said both the Roman and the Galatian were wrong. "Those disciples were speaking plain ordinary Aramaic. They sounded as though they had one drink too many — and maybe the centurion did, too," commented one shopkeeper who asked that his name not be used. He said he had closed and barricaded his shop because of the size of the crowd at the temple porch and the fear that some trouble might erupt.

Barsabbas Jona, a marriage broker and counselor whose booth is located near the temple, said that many of those in the crowd were pilgrims here for the festival. They reacted emotionally to the pleadings of the Galileans, he said, and probably responded with doxologies in their own language.

Peter the Fisherman towered head and shoulders above the others and seemed to be the chief speaker, Barsabbas said. Making a fervent plea for converts, Peter urged the crowd, "Save yourselves from this crooked generation. Believe and repent so that you can be baptized." In response, "several thousand people" pledged that they would join the Nazarene's fellowship, Barsabbas stated.

Rabbi Joab said no effort had been made to halt the meeting since it is the custom of the High Priest to open the gates of the temple at sundown on the eve of a holy day so worshipers could enter and prepare for their sacrifices.

Thoughts

(for personal reflection or group discussion)

1. When we have a lot to do and are in a hurry, some of us might think it all right to skip prayers. Yet Luther once remarked that when he faced a very busy day, he needed to spend twice the normal amount of time in prayer. Which is the better idea, and why?

2. Some people claim that a common language for all mankind would bring about world peace. Relate this to the events at Pentecost.

3. In our democratic election process, contests are decided after strenuous campaigning and vote-getting. None of this leaves room for divine intervention and for seeking God's will. Compare this with the method used by the disciples, who prayed and cast lots.

Questions

1. What meaning do you see in the fact that the disciples were fervently engaged in prayer when the Holy Spirit's power descended on them?

2. What is the meaning of wind and fire as symbols of the Holy Spirit?

3. What happened to the money Judas got to betray Jesus?

4. Who was chosen to succeed Judas?

5. How were sermons and speeches preserved in biblical times?

6. What was the result of Peter's preaching at Pentecost?

Chapter 4

At the Beautiful Gate

Read Acts 2:43—4:31

The disciples remained together at Jerusalem after Pentecost, devoting themselves to teaching those who had been added to their little band. While 3,000 may have been baptized at Pentecost, the logic of the situation makes one wonder how such a mass baptism could have taken place. The figure seems more likely to have been cumulative over a period of time.

The followers of Jesus were not at this time called Christians, but were spoken of rather as the Sect of the Nazarenes or sometimes as Followers of the Way. The group formed a typical sectarian synagogue, such as had gathered around prophets at various times in the history of Israel. Many prophets in Israel had rebelled against the formal religious organization headed by the official priestly leadership, but still considered themselves within Judaism. Like them, the disciples had no intention of separating themselves from the Jewish community or the traditional Jewish faith, but they believed that they possessed a special insight into God's plan for the Jews, his people. Their distinctive doctrine was that the long-expected Messiah had come in the person of Jesus and had revealed himself to them. They therefore bound themselves together in a loving relationship because they understood that this was in the spirit of the Messiah, who had commanded them to love one another.

All Things in Common

This company of believers had certain rituals and practices which set them apart from other synagogue groups. Not only were they unified by their spirit of mutual love and good feeling, which would in those days have been a sufficient mark of distinction, but they even shared all their possessions. In this sense, they were "communists" in the very best connotation of that word, for they enjoyed a kind of communal living which can succeed only when the whole group is of one heart and mind. Another group which attempted such a lifestyle in those days was the Essenes. However, human nature is such that this kind of living, based on mutual affection and utter unselfishness, can endure only for a little while. Even in recent times separatist groups have attempted this style, usually as an exercise in Christian love, but when the novelty wears off their experiment is doomed.

These early Christians renounced their worldly possessions and gave up their personal goods (2:44-46 and 4:32-37), so that the poor shared equally with those who were formerly rich. While the needy were cared for in all early Christian communities, this experiment in communal living seems to have been only in Jerusalem. Special mention is given to Joseph Barnabas, a Levite and a native of Cyprus, who sold a valuable property when he joined the community and donated the proceeds to the fund which was held for common use.

Another mark of this early church was that they devoted themselves to worship and to preaching. Here again we see that they regarded themselves as a unique sect within the Jewish framework, however, for they attended the temple together (2:46) and then added their own ritual of breaking bread together in their homes. (2:42-47) Apparently they engaged in this kind of devotion full time, similar to monastic orders in later years. They had left their business to follow Jesus and did not go back into their trades afterward. This in itself must have hastened the end of their idyllic post-ascension period, for inevitably the time would come when money would run out and when new converts did not bring in enough new funds to provide the necessaries of life for a growing community.

Their preaching at this time seems to have been patterned after Peter's sermon on Pentecost, described as a "testimony to the resurrection of Jesus." Peter had then retold the story of redemption. God had prepared the way for Jesus throughout the whole history of the Jewish nation, sending his revelations even when people were too blind or too thickheaded to comprehend it. Then when the time came and the eyes of the people were ready to be opened to the fullness of light, God sent his Son to fulfill prophecy and to be the Messiah and Savior of the Jews.

Naturally as the news of this unusual community spread, rumors abounded about the power of the apostles. Many sick people were brought to them for help and they were able to respond with "signs and wonders," healing many illnesses. It got to the point where people thronged around the disciples whenever they walked through the streets, hoping for the chance to see some miracle if just the shadow of Peter might fall on them. The quality of life displayed by the disciples and their followers was such that they were held in high honor. Even strangers from outlying towns brought in their sick and "those afflicted with unclean spirits" so that the apostles might heal them.

A Miracle of Healing

While Luke has few supporting details from this period, he does tell about the healing of the lame beggar at the Gate Beautiful of the temple. It is a story of great charm and deep meaning.

Miracles in the Bible are always recorded for a purpose. This lovely story has as its setting the entrance to the holiest shrine of the Jews, a place where beggars would congregate because people going in to worship might feel inclined to quiet a guilty conscience by giving them alms. Those who have travelled in the Holy Land know that such beggars still operate today in much the same way. Holding out a pathetically thin hand, they will call out, "American! Give money!" Today, as in biblical times, begging is an honorable profession for some of these people. Every day of their lives they come to the same place, as though they held a lease on it, sitting in their rags and pleading for gifts from passers-by.

The man whom Peter helped had a very good spot for begging. He was carried there every day and occupied a privileged position at the Gate Beautiful. This was one of nine gates that led into the inner court of the temple, the area from which foreigners and gentiles were barred on pain of death. Four gates were on the north side, four on the south, and the ninth gate, the Gate Beautiful, faced eastward toward the Kidron Valley and the Mount of Olives. This gate reportedly required a staff of twenty men to swing it open each morning and to close it at sundown.

Here the lame man waited to ask alms of any who passed through to enter the temple. Maybe relatives or friends carried him there each day, or maybe he had colleagues with whom he "shared the wealth." In any event, he was a familiar figure to all those in Jerusalem.

As Peter and John came by, they paid particular attention to the lame man. Peter "directed his gaze at him," stopping to look more closely than usual at the beggar. Obviously they had seen the beggar many times before and perhaps the beggar recognized them. But this time Peter said to the lame man, "Look at us." Of course, the lame man obeyed. He looked at them eagerly. He expected to get something good and was eager to receive it. Maybe it would be a gold piece, surely at least a silver coin. But then Peter said to him, "Silver and gold have I none, but such as I have I give to you. In the name of Jesus Christ of Nazareth, arise and walk." Peter then took him by the hand and raised him up and immediately his feet and ankles were made strong!

The lame beggar's reaction was natural. A tingling new experience was coming into his life. He was standing unassisted, without a crutch or helper. His dormant muscles were beginning to flex. He tested them with great joy, "walking and leaping and praising God." A wonderful gift had just been given to him and he reacted exuberantly.

Note especially what Peter said: "Silver and gold have I none." That's a condition we often claim to be in. Even our coins today are not silver and gold. There may be some nickel and copper, but nothing more precious. What do we possess that's more important? Certainly one answer would be, our faith in God and in the power of God that flows through us.

Peter believed that, but this event must have been a test for his faith, too. Peter was not accustomed to being a miracle worker. There were signs and wonders done by the apostles, but this is the first time they put their power to test in public and the first time we have full details of a miracle. They had seen Jesus call down the power of God upon people who needed miraculous help. But only after Pentecost, with the coming of the Spirit's power into their lives, did they dare to feel that perhaps somehow they might also draw upon that power to aid others. So Peter was testing himself and also testing God. Suppose nothing had happened? Suppose the lame man had attempted to rise but had fallen back into a heap again? Peter could have felt that he had tried, that he had done as much as he could. Doctors don't always cure their patients; prayers are not always granted (they may be *answered* without being granted); so how can one expect a miracle?

But this worked. Peter said, "In the name of Jesus Christ of Nazareth arise and walk." That was the formula for receiving power.

Jesus had once told the disciples, "Whatever you ask in my name . . ." Now the apostles knew the truth of this promise. Because they had been filled with power by the Holy Spirit, they could transmit that power to others!

The miracle had the effect that one would expect. Evidently Peter and John went to Solomon's Portico, a place where they met daily with the other disciples to teach and pray. Meanwhile the word spread like wildfire around the temple that the well-known cripple who begged daily at the door had been healed. People were astonished and rushed to see if the report was true. They saw with their own eyes the man who had been healed. He "clung to Peter and John." And why not? They had changed his life. And when "all the people" had run together to Solomon's Porch, Peter seized the opportunity to deliver another sermon, very similar in content to the sermon at Pentecost. Again it had a great effect. This time it was supported not by speaking in tongues but by the visible transformation of a helpless cripple into a person who could walk and leap.

The commotion attracted the priests and the temple guard, with the result that Peter and John were arrested. This was the first of numerous occasions when disciples were taken into custody and then used the opportunity to proclaim the message about Jesus. The next day Peter and John were hauled before the "rulers and elders and scribes" and ordered to explain how they dared to disturb the peace of the temple. The learned rabbis and scribes must have been taken somewhat aback by the spirited defense put up by Peter, an "uneducated common man." But they had also known for years about the affliction of the beggar who had been healed and who now stood erect alongside the disciples as living proof of the miracle. What could they say to this? After conferring with one another, the council members decided only to warn the disciples to stop preaching and teaching about Jesus. Emboldened anew, Peter then defied them with his answer: "Is it right to listen to you rather than to listen to God? We must speak of what we have seen and heard!" Today, Peter might have said, "We have to tell it like it is."

44

From the Jerusalem *Post*
Kislev 4, 3794 (December 1, A.D. 33)

"We Didn't Do It — God Did," Says Peter, But Priests Order Him Held For Trial

A quiet afternoon at the Gate Beautiful nearly turned into a riot late yesterday after two members of the Nazarene cult reportedly healed a lame beggar. A large crowd quickly gathered and refused to break up until after dark when Peter the Fisherman and John ben Zebedee were taken into protective custody by temple guards.

Tocholas, the man who was said to have been healed, is widely known in Jerusalem and to pilgrims who have come to the temple in recent years. Unable to walk since his birth forty years ago, Tocholas has been a familiar figure for many years to those who use the Gate Beautiful, usually occupying the same spot on the steps. Some pilgrims go out of their way to give him a token, since they believe that this will bring them good luck and a safe homeward journey.

Yesterday Tocholas was at his accustomed place when the two disciples approached. He made his usual appeal for alms, but Peter reportedly stated that he had no money, but would give him something better. According to onlookers, he then reached down and lifted Tocholas to his feet. The lame man then suddenly began leaping in the air and walking and running normally. His shouts quickly attracted a crowd.

Temple guards who pushed their way through the throng said they found Tocholas on his knees, holding on to Peter and shouting "Hallelujah!" Knowing that he was a cripple, the guards tried to clear a space for him to lie down, but Tocholas instead began jumping up and down shouting.

Scribe Peseach of the temple staff was summoned by the guards. "If Tocholas has been feigning lameness for these years, he must answer for his deceit," Peseach announced to the crowd. "If on the other hand these Nazarenes are responsible for the so-called healing, they will be charged with witchcraft and will answer to the council."

Peter immediately silenced the scribe. "What makes you think that we by our own powers or holiness made this man walk?" he demanded. "The God of Abraham and Isaac and Jacob, the God of our fathers, has glorified his son Jesus, and faith in the name of Jesus is the power that has made this man strong and has given him sound limbs again."

Some persons in the crowd threatened Peseach and the temple guards led him to safety. Peter then climbed onto the wall around Solomon's Porch and launched into a long discourse about the Nazarene prophet whom sect members claim was raised from the dead. "Repent and be converted, that your sins may be blotted out through Jesus Christ," Peter exhorted. Many in the crowd took up the chant, answering "We repent! We believe."

The density of the crowd made it impossible for those who wanted to enter the temple for the evening sacrifice to get through. The chief priests, Annas and Caiaphas, therefore ordered the temple guard to break up the demonstration by placing Peter and John under arrest on charges of disturbing the temple services.

"Unrecognized teachers have no right to preach in the temple courtyard," said the Sadducee lawyer Ben-Zaled. He also took issue with Peter's talk about the resurrection, terming it "unacceptable and heretic." His statement led to another minor flare-up as Shemuel the Pharisee took issue with him.

"You are angry because you deny any resurrection and these people say Jesus was resurrected," he declared. "The resurrection story is harmless nonsense, but you have no right to prevent any prophet from speaking freely in the temple courts so long as he does it in fear of the great God of our fathers."

The Pharisee added the charge which has recently been debated in the Sanhedrin, that the Sadducee party was growing wealthy on the temple trade and was not paying its full share into the temple treasury.

The guards had to be called back to break up the argument. Peter and John were detained in the temple prison for the night, since the priests ruled that they will have to appear before the Sanhedrin this morning to answer any charges that may be brought against them and also to explain their actions in allegedly healing Tocholas.

"We will welcome the chance to testify before the Sanhedrin about the power of Jesus Christ to heal bodies and souls," Peter said. Shemuel the Pharisee, who is a member of the Sanhedrin, said he had grave doubts about the so-called miracle, but that he would insist that Tocholas testify at the trial as a material witness and that the Nazarenes be given the right to have their own lawyers present.

Thoughts

(for personal reflection or group discussion)

1. "Be careful when you pray. God may give you what you ask for." How does this saying relate to the condition of the lame beggar at the Beautiful Gate?

2. Often we respond to appeals for help by giving money. Are there alternative ways? Do you find that it is usually easier to give money to a good cause than to devote time and energy to it? What's better for a congregation, to have members sing in the choir or to have members give money so paid singers can be hired?

3. The temple priests were not pleased by the healing of the lame beggar. Do we sometimes also react negatively to the good fortune of others? Have you ever been upset because someone else got a job or honor that you wanted? Were you justified?

Questions

1. What special characteristic marked the Christian community in Jerusalem?

2. What words made Peter's statement to the lame beggar effective?

3. What results came from the healing of the lame beggar?

4. How did Peter take advantage of the uproar caused by the healing?

5. What was the secret of Peter's power? Why can't Christians today have the power to heal others?

Chapter 5

Mysterious Deaths

Read Acts 4:32—5:11

The Christians in Jerusalem "held everything in common." This practice was communism in the good sense of the word, a word that has a nasty connotation to many in the world today. What is called "communism" today is not really communism. It is a political system which should rightly be called state socialism. In the Union of Soviet Socialist Republics (the USSR), the people don't share equally in the land, the wealth or the power. True communism would require such sharing. However, only a small ruling clique in the USSR has the right to decide what share an individual may have. In contrast the early Christians shared all things equally with one another.

Naturally, we wonder why. What did they gain by selling their land and putting the proceeds into a common pot? Wouldn't those who owned property be better equipped to manage the money and to dole out what was needed by others? Common sharing seems sometimes to subsidize the lazy and careless persons and to penalize the prudent, hardworking ones. On the other side, the argument for private ownership is that individuals take better care of their own things and manage them more efficiently.

The Problem of Human Nature

It's hard to see how a system of common ownership could work in a Christian congregation today. Sometimes congregations try to operate their organizations on this principle, with mixed results. Such congregations adopt a policy that all congregational organizations must put their funds into a common treasury. The money is then held in a central fund and whenever a need arises, an organization can draw on this fund, according to this theory. And what an outcry is usually made! "The church council is trying to take our money," they cry.

A little church in Florida adopted this plan. They informed all organizations that whatever money they collected through dues or other means should be put into a common fund and whatever was needed would be paid out of that fund. All the groups went along except the Altar Guild. Those women said, "Oh, no you don't! We get the money for altar flowers and we've been self-supporting all along and we're not going to put our money in with anybody else's to pay for someone else's functions!"

Since this is a normal reaction in any group, we wonder why the Christians in Jerusalem ever tried this experiment. It must have been that they really had such love and concern for one another that they trusted each other completely. This goes beyond what's normally possible even in a family circle. Each member of a family unit likes to have his own bank account or at least his own piggy bank. In most families, common sharing would be difficult at best. Some examples may indeed exist, but others would feel it a great invasion of privacy if they had to ask for every nickel and thus disclose to the whole family how each nickel was spent. There are also less mature members of a family who would waste the communal resources if they had equal access to them. We can easily think of dozens of barriers to this kind of sharing and understanding, but perhaps this is what love is all about. Perhaps love is really the ability to say without reservation, "What is mine is yours and I hold nothing back from you." It's a lofty stage of human relationships, but they obviously attained it in the early church, or at least came close to attaining it.

We have to add a reservation, because there were exceptions and because the system lasted for only a short time. One such exception is recorded in its entirety and in great detail. One wonders why Luke included so negative a story in his narrative, but it is included because the Bible is an honest book and Luke was an honest reporter. Even in the Old Testament, the defeats are listed as well as the victories. This stands out in vivid contrast to other ancient histories. In the annals of most ancient lands, the rulers strictly ordered their scribes to list only the favorable events. But because humankind knows both good and evil, the Bible records the favorable and the unfavorable, the good and the bad. The Bible does not shrink from telling us the truth, from the serpent in Eden to those in the idyllic early Christian community who could not give themselves whole-heartedly to the cause.

Ananias and Sapphira

While almost everybody willingly contributed all they had to the common treasury, a man named Ananias and his wife Sapphira had sold a piece of property, but had conspired to withhold a part of the proceeds. Evidently Ananias was the sly one, but he acted "with his wife's knowledge," so she was also implicated. It is clear from the story that there was no pressure on Ananias to sell the property. It belonged to him and he had the full right to keep it. The communal system in which the Christians shared was not forced by any kind of law, but only by love.

Ananias could have said, "This property is ours and we will keep it since we can support ourselves and don't need anybody's help." But instead he took upon himself the obligation of sharing with the group. He therefore sold the property, but contrary to his pledge he brought only a part of the proceeds to lay at the apostles' feet. His sin, according to Peter, was "to lie to the Holy Spirit. You have not lied to men but to God."

When Ananias heard these words, he fell down and died. It's rather a strange story, because it says that the young men then wrapped him up and carried him out and buried him without even telling his wife about it. When Sapphira came onto the scene about three hours later, Peter confronted her not with words of comfort because of the death of her husband, but rather with an accusation: "Tell me how much you sold that land for!" When she responded by giving the figure upon which she and her husband had agreed, Peter immediately indicted her and proclaimed her doom. "You have agreed to tempt the Lord . . . those who buried your husband are at the door and they will carry you out."

Immediately poor Sapphira fell down and died, without the op-portunity to say a word in her own defense. Her body was then carried out to be buried beside her husband. No wonder a great fear fell on all! And what a story for the newspapers!

It's hard to see much love in this treatment of Ananias and Sap-phira, even though they were liars and conspirators. The event seems more like the judgment of a harsh god of justice than the compas-sionate actions of followers of a Lord of love.

50

Yet Jesus himself had warned the disciples to remain constantly alert to guard against evil, which would worm its way into the group if they permitted it. So even this small and closeknit group who loved one another so dearly had to stay alert lest somebody take advantage of their innocence. Love dare not be blind. Sometimes love is best demonstrated by discipline and chastisement. If parents find that their child is becoming a slave to a drug habit or is breaking the law, love requires that they take corrective action.

Christians are told to go the second mile and to offer one's shirt also when someone steals your coat. But on our city streets today there are plenty of people ready to steal a coat and we need not be too willing to add the shirt. Rather, we holler for the police. There are times when, in spite of our ideals and our willingness to put the best construction on the actions of others, we need to be on guard against those who would take advantage of our situation. The story of Ananias and Sapphira stands therefore as a warning to Christians to beware of those who by guile seek to impose upon them or exploit them. Even though we love and trust our fellow church members, it's a good idea to carry insurance and to require a bond for the treasurer. It's nothing personal, but Jesus advised us to be as "wise as serpents" because we are often like sheep in the midst of wolves!

From the Jerusalem *Post*
Tebet 21, 3796 (January 10, A.D. 36)

Mystery Surrounds Sudden Deaths Of Local Couple At Church Meeting

Police today continued questioning witnesses in the bizarre deaths of a man and his wife at a religious meeting held here yesterday. Ananias, a wealthy local landowner, and his wife Sapphira died within three hours of each other. In both cases there was no evidence of violence and police listed the cause of death as "sudden shock."

No marks were found on the body of either victim, according to Centurion Quirinius of the inner city detail. Despite rigorous questioning by police, all those present at the meeting of the Nazarene sect where the deaths occurred said the victims fell dead suddenly, making no outcry and without being touched by anyone. In both cases, however, the victims had been talking with Simon Peter, a Galilean fisherman who is the local leader of the sect.

"We have no evidence that

will permit us to place a charge against Peter," Quirinius told reporters. "His story that he did not touch or attack the pair dovetails with that of witnesses. Since there is no trace of poison, we have been compelled to list the cause of death as unknown."

One of Peter's associates claimed that the couple had been "stricken by God" because they told lies. He said that just before the deaths occurred, there had been a dispute about the value of some property which Ananias recently sold on behalf of the sect, which consists of followers of the late Jesus of Nazareth. Jesus was a prophet and rabbi who was crucified here four years ago by the Romans, who charged him with subversion. His followers claim that Jesus returned to life and is still living somewhere outside the city.

The Nazarenes have been active in the real estate market in recent months. Joseph Barnabas, a Levite from Cyprus and a recent convert to the group, sold a large field just west of the city a short time ago. Funds from such sales by members are said to have been placed in a general fund for the benefit of the whole group and are distributed by a ruling committee of elders to those in need.

Ananias came to the weekly meeting of the sect yesterday in order to make a contribution to this fund, Peter said. The money came from sale of property jointly held by Ananias and his wife. Tax records indicate that the property was sold for thirty shekels. Police refused to state whether this money had been found.

Witnesses said that Ananias came into the room where the meeting was being held and put some coins on the floor in front of the elders of the sect. Peter then sprang to his feet and accused Ananias of deceit, saying that he had "kept back part of the proceeds of the land." Without responding, Ananias collapsed and died instantly.

The Roman guard said their suspicion was aroused because young men at the meeting immediately wrapped the body of Ananias in burial strips, carried it to the cemetery and placed it in the family tomb. Although Jewish law requires burial before nightfall, the Romans insist on examining a body if death is believed to have occurred through foul play or violence.

The death of Sapphira followed a similar pattern. She arrived at the meeting about three hours after the death of her husband. When told of his sudden demise, she fell to the floor. It is not known if efforts were made to revive her, but one of the women in the group said that the double tragedy had cast such fear on those present that they were "just like paralyzed."

Burial of Sapphira took place in the family tomb alongside her husband. The couple had no children.

Ananias, who was more than forty years old, was a native of Jerusalem. He gained attention two years ago when he led a protest demonstration at a meeting of the Sanhedrin against an increase in temple taxes. He said at that time that as a property owner and landlord he found the triple taxation by Rome, by the city and by the temple an intolerable burden. He later withdrew his membership from the synagogue and joined the Nazarene sect.

In a brief funeral address, Peter said that Ananias "died before he came to our meeting." When Satan entered into his heart and broke the bond of fellowship and trust that must exist among the followers of Jesus, his spirit actually died, according to Peter.

"The death of the body was a natural result, but it was not as important as the separation of the spirit from God which had taken place earlier," the sect leader added. He quoted words of Jesus that "whoever plans evil in his heart has already sinned."

Thoughts

(for personal reflection or group discussion)

1. Groups of Christians in the early nineteenth century established communal or socialist colonies where they held all things in common, evidently in emulation of the early Christians in Jerusalem. Among such groups were the Oneida community in New York, Zoar in Ohio, Amana in Iowa, New Harmony in Indiana and Brook Farm in Massachusetts. All of them failed. Why?

2. To what extent does my congregation allow equality among all members? Are some members given special attention because they contribute more generously?

3. The family is the ideal place for sharing. How does my family stack up in this regard? Are they cheerful sharers? Do they trust one another? What amount of sharing can we reasonably strive for?

4. Ananias and Sapphira evidently conspired together to conceal the value of their property. Was conspiracy the sin worthy of death? If not, what was their real sin?

Questions

1. Why did Luke include the Ananias' story in his narrative?

2. Did not Ananias have a right to his own property, to do with it what he wanted?

3. Since women had little right to make financial decisions, was it right for Sapphira to suffer a fate equal to her husband's?

4. Was the verdict pronounced by Peter in conformity with our ideas of Christian love and mercy? Didn't God say, "Vengeance is mine"?

5. Does love ever require or include punishment? For example, does a parent ever punish a child because he or she loves the child?

Chapter 6

The First Martyr

Read Acts 5:12—8:1

For about five years after the resurrection of Jesus, the disciples were content to remain in Jerusalem. Jesus had told them to wait there and they seemed to feel that they were limited to this place. Because they were all Jews, they formed their own "synagogue" or religious organization. Outsiders identified them by various names, such as the "Sect of the Nazarenes," but they preferred to call themselves simply followers of "The Way."

Accustomed as we are to highly organized and bureaucratic church organizations, we may have difficulty appreciating the informality which prevailed in those days. Formal Jewish worship was centered in the temple, the place of sacrifice and the "House of God." Temple worship was ruled by the high priests, who were however appointed and removed by the reigning king or by alien governors. All good Jews were supposed to come to the temple at certain times for ritual sacrifice, worship and praise.

Alongside the temple, synagogue worship had established itself. For most people, it was in the synagogue that they read the Law, listened to learned rabbis and provided for the education of their children. It required only ten or more persons to organize a synagogue, so even in small towns there could be a locally-controlled congregation. Elected to administer its affairs were "elders" or "rulers," called a Sanhedrin. In big cities like Jerusalem, this group consisted of twenty-three members, but in small towns there were usually seven. In Jerusalem there were said to be 480 synagogues. Some were formed by special-interest groups; Acts 6:9 lists four or five of this kind. Therefore one more synagogue composed of friends and followers of Jesus would scarcely be noticed.

During this period of patience and inaction in Jerusalem, the number of believers in Jesus grew. We read of 3,000 being added as members at one time and of 5,000 at another time. These numbers may be symbolic, for no such large numbers of people joined the inner circle. It was still possible for the entire company of believers to gather in the houses of members.

Staying Close to Home

During this period the disciples seem to have overlooked completely the mandate of Jesus that they were to carry his message to the ends of the world. They did not reach out, nor did they feel any qualms of conscience because they were not going forth into the world. They remained a typical sectarian synagogue group, a unique sect within the framework of Judaism, such as had gathered at various times around prophets or rabbis. They had no intention of separating from the Jewish community or the Jewish religion.

Since Jews of various nationalities or of differing doctrinal concepts were permitted to gather freely on Solomon's Portico, outside the temple, they took advantage of this to conduct meetings where they could witness to Jews from other parts of the world who had come as pilgrims to Jerusalem. They also attended the temple, like other loyal Jews. They would then return to their own homes or to some central residence for their own special ritual of breaking bread together in remembrance of Jesus.

While Luke mentions the "whole church" (in Greek, *ecclesia*) in 5:11, this term may have been used at the time when Luke wrote his account. The Jewishness of those early years seems better indicated by their designation as the "Synagogue of the Nazarenes," a term that is used in some early Christian writings.

The general peacefulness of this period was broken by several unhappy events, such as the failure of Ananias and Sapphira to live up to the standards of the group. Certainly the sudden calamity which befell those two gave the others something to think about! It broke the circle of trust which had knit the group together and must have aroused suspicions. If one such falsifier was among them, might there not be others? After all, with the growth in numbers there is also a loosening of ties. It is easier to have personal faith in a few hundred people than in a few thousand. Even today, small congregations are likely to be closeknit and perhaps even interrelated, while in large churches many members have only a passing acquaintance with one another and are held together primarily by their mutual interest in the congregation and in the sharing of the Gospel.

A second source of trouble as the group grew larger came from the widows. The early Christians had a deep concern for desolate "real widows," as Paul later related. (1 Timothy 5:3-16) Widows with children were to be cared for by their families and "younger widows" were to marry and bear children, but those who are childless and over sixty years of age were the responsibility of their Christian friends, according to Paul.

In the Jerusalem church, the widows of Greeks said they were not getting the same portion of food as the widows of Jews, or something like that. It was a typical squabble over a minor feeling of hurt, but when the disciples heard about it, they were troubled. What should they do? Maybe their group was becoming so large as to be unmanageable. It was losing its harmony and cliques or parties were evidently developing. As a result of this incident, the Twelve elected seven others, who were to be elders or presbyters and who would assist the apostles in serving tables to see that everyone got a fair amount.

The Death of Stephen

Among the elected elders were two whose names are etched deeply into Christian history — Philip and Stephen. Stephen immediately stepped into a leading role among the religious community of Jerusalem. He did signs and wonders among the people. He was a gifted speaker and attracted crowds to his preaching. His popularity grew so rapidly that members of other synagogues became alarmed and plotted together against Stephen. They tried to argue and dispute with him, but his strength of conviction and his debating skills were too much for them. When they could not successfully counter his arguments, they hauled him into court where they accused him of preaching and teaching against the laws of Moses.

Stephen's response to this charge was remarkable. Instead of defending himself, he went on the attack. Like an ancient prophet, he reviewed the history of Israel, chiding the Jews for always turning deaf ears to God's warnings and for refusing to accept the signs which God had sent. Their final rejection was the betrayal and murder of the Righteous One, Jesus.

"You stiff-necked people, uncircumcised in heart and ears, you always resist the Holy Spirit!" Stephen thundered. Probably he recognized that the court would find him guilty regardless of what he said, so rather than pull his punches or try to be conciliatory he really let them have it. The result was that they all became enraged and "ground their teeth against him." This curious custom of hissing and gnashing teeth was a symbol among the Jews of extreme distaste and loathing.

Refusing to listen any longer to Stephen's sermon, they then "stopped their ears" and cast him down to be stoned to death. The followers of Jesus had their first martyr.

The stoning of Stephen made it clear to the Christians that they were no longer safe at Jerusalem. Their bold and open advocacy of the lordship of Jesus and their success in winning converts had stirred up deepseated opposition. So long as their opponents simply murmured and grumbled, the Christians were able to go about their ways without concern. But now that physical attacks were being made, the lives and property of the entire community were in danger. The continuation of their peaceful program of worship and praise was impossible. Also, by this time their experiment of holding all their possessions in common seems to have come to an end.

Evil events can sometimes lead to a good result. In this case, the tragic death of one of their leaders and the sudden change of atmosphere which it produced compelled the disciples to re-examine their plan of action. As a small synagogue in Jerusalem, they had been able to conduct their affairs safely within the protection of the Jewish community, but now the Jews themselves were reacting violently against them. New strategy was needed.

The Scattering of the Faithful

The martyrdom of Stephen therefore became the catalyst which forced the followers of The Way to venture out into new areas. Although Jerusalem remained a sort of headquarters for Christians at least until the destruction of the city in A.D. 70, many fled from the city to seek safer quarters in neighboring towns and villages, leaving only a small core group to remain with the Twelve. Some went to Samaria, perhaps in fulfilment of what Jesus had said just before the ascension ("You shall be my witnesses in Jerusalem and in all Judea and in Samaria . . .").

As they went away from Jerusalem, they began to reach out to some who were not Jews — Samaritans, for instance. Hesitatingly and even unwillingly, Christians were forced to take their Gospel out into the unknown and insecure surroundings of the gentile and pagan world. And while the Jerusalem church continued as a sort of synagogue community, restricted by Jewish laws, the others no longer felt confined to the Jewish mold. Their dispersion thus brought a bonus to the church. Wherever they went, they told the story of Jesus and preached the Word. The Gospel reached a new constituency.

Thoughts

(for personal reflection or group discussion)

1. People tend to become content with the status quo, the way things are. "Experience shows that mankind is more disposed to suffer evils than to right them," Thomas Jefferson wrote. He thought that frequent revolutions are needed. How does that apply to the church? To your congregation?

2. Some people feel at home in a large congregation while others feel more at home in the intimacy of a small (or even exclusive) one. What advantages or drawbacks do you see in being part of a large congregation? A small one? Is there an ideal size?

3. What limits must we place on open criticism of those who disagree with us?

Questions

1. Were there different sects or denominations among the Jews?

2. Did Jerusalem have many synagogues?

3. What names were given to the early followers of Jesus before they were called Christians?

4. How did Stephen characterize people who refused to believe in Jesus?

5. What happened to the followers of Jesus after the stoning of Stephen?

Chapter 7

On to Samaria

Read Acts 8:2-40

Among those who went out from Jerusalem was Philip, another of the seven new elders. His pioneer spirit led him to Samaria, a region north of Jerusalem, and a hard field for a Jew to work. Samaritan people were regarded by the Jews as outcasts and apostates. Although they were Semitic, like the Jews, they had through intermarriage become a mixed race. They worshiped the God of Abraham and followed the laws of Moses, but their worship centered around Mount Gerizim rather than the temple at Jerusalem. They refused to acknowledge the authority of the high priests.

Jesus himself had come under criticism for teaching and ministering to Samaritans. In one striking example, he deliberately made a hero of a Samaritan in one of his parables in order to contrast the kindness of this religious outcast with the snobbish and indifferent behavior of the Jewish priest and Levite. The priest and Levite represented classes of Jews who considered themselves to have attained the highest degree of religious perfection.

The Samaritans help us understand the divergencies that existed among Jews. No large group is ever completely monolithic. Jews were divided by the intensity of their religious devotion and also by geographical and cultural background. Then as now, some Jews were devout and fanatical people who tried to observe all the laws of Moses and of their rabbis, an almost impossible task which would have occupied every movement in their lives. Then there was a great body of Jews who kept the festivals and obeyed the basic laws, but not so strictly. And there were also Jews who simply disregarded religious observances. Within the Jewish fold there were also sects such as Pharisees, Sadducees and Essenes who quarreled with one another over various doctrines and observances. But all Jews who looked to the temple at Jerusalem as the center for their religion had one thing in common — they despised the Samaritans and regarded them as heretics.

Philip went to a city in Samaria where he boldly preached the Gospel and found that many responded readily to his teaching about Jesus. While the Samaritans accepted as their religious authority only the five books of Moses, the Pentateuch, they awaited the coming of a prophet like Moses and may even have had some Messianic hope. They expressed great joy when Philip's message assured them that they were included in God's plan of salvation through his Son, Jesus.

Philip Meets "Simon the Great"

Philip's remarkable success as an evangelist among the Samaritans was climaxed when he converted a notorious local celebrity, a magician or sorcerer who billed himself as "Simon the Great." Magicians seem always to like to identify themselves as "the Great." In days when superstitious people were ready to believe that magic was a display of the power of God, this appellation had some meaning.

Philip's message struck home to Simon, who allowed himself to be baptized. The depth of his conversion is uncertain, because a little later we find him trying to bribe the disciples to reveal to him the secret of the Holy Spirit's power. But among the Samaritans Simon's conversion must have seemed a nine-day wonder, and when Simon testified publicly to his faith in Jesus, it surely had great influence among the common people.

The conversion of Simon was like an early ray of sunrise. Mornings when I have stirred early enough to see the sun rise and the dawn lighten the sky, I have been impressed by the fact that it does not come suddenly, like one great flash of lightning or one great burst of light. The first sign of dawn is a slight grayness in the eastern sky, followed by a brighter light, perhaps with a few pinkish fingers stretching out from the spot where the sun is about to come above the horizon. Then perhaps a cloud catches one of those early beams of light like a pink ball of cotton, and finally there is a brightening orange glow that precedes the moment of sunrise.

The spread of the Christian faith as the Bible reveals it to us is something like such a sunrise. First there was the grayness, then a finger reaching out here and there. Philip's preaching was such a finger pointing toward Simon, who considered himself something great. A little later we read of Philip's message reaching out to another special person.

News of what was happening in Samaria got back to Jerusalem in a hurry. Maybe it caused consternation among Saul and his band of persecutors, but they were stiff-necked Jews and felt little concern about what was happening in Samaria. But the news also caused a stir among the disciples, so Peter and John decided to come up to see what was happening. They may have had a hard time convincing themselves that Samaria was the place where God would plant his church, but they must also have remembered that Jesus treated Samaritans as friends and ministered to them. Their eyes must have been opened by the fact that the Gospel could reach out beyond the confines of Judaism to people who were considered by the Jews as second-class citizens.

When Does the Holy Spirit Come?

With the arrival of Peter and John, the ministry to the Samaritans took on a new dimension. For some reason, the Samaritans had not received the Holy Spirit, although they had been baptized by Philip in the name of the Lord Jesus. When the two apostles joined the mission, they laid hands on people who then received the Spirit. This raises an interesting question, for it seems contrary to all the doctrines about baptism. It seems to be the only instance where the rite of baptism and the indwelling of the Spirit are separated. It may have been this peculiar incident which gave rise in later Christianity to a separation of baptism and confirmation. In liturgical churches (Roman Catholic, Episcopal, Lutheran), the priest or pastor baptizes (or in an emergency, any Christian) but the rite of confirmation with its laying on of hands is administered usually by a bishop. This is one of those cases where you can snip a little incident out of the Bible to support a doctrinal position. Taken in full context and with acceptance of the underlying principle, it is clear that the Holy Spirit is not bound by any particular ritual or practice. There are instances where the power of the Holy Spirit filled people when they heard the Word of God, when they received the laying-on of hands, or when they were baptized. The doctrines of churches are indeed important, but they never provide a straitjacket for the power of God. As Paul later wrote, "There are differences of administration, but the same Spirit."

The inflow of the Spirit's power by the laying-on of hands caused a minor conflict. When Simon the Magician, the newly-won convert, became aware of the power that was being given to others, he confronted the apostles with a proposition. He offered them money if he could in return have the apostolic power to lay hands on people and convey to them the power of the Spirit. Peter rebuked him sharply, saying, "This is a wicked offer. Your silver perish with you if you think you can obtain the power of God with money. Your heart is not right — repent!" Simon was not fazed by this, for he boldly suggested that the disciples ought to pray for him so that no evil would come upon him because of his effort to bribe them.

One result of this incident was to give Simon a sort of immortality, for the word "simony," which means the buying or selling of a church office or ecclesiastical preferment, lives on in our language today!

The team of Peter, John and Philip continued their missionary ministry in Samaria for some time before returning to Jerusalem. But Philip was soon on the move again. His special work was not yet complete. He had reached out to the Samaritans, a tiny step toward extending the Gospel and reaching out to the world. Now he was to move in a different direction, to the south of Jerusalem, and to a more exotic piece of mission work.

Baptism of the Queen's Treasurer

On the road from Jerusalem to Gaza, which passes through the northwest corner of the Sinai desert, Philip encountered a chariot bearing an Ethiopian, a black man, who was treasurer for Queen Candace and therefore highly placed in his nation. The fact that he was traveling by chariot attests to his wealth and position. Only the rich could ride! And a chariot was the speediest form of transportation, being drawn by a horse and often used as a war weapon. The finest chariots were made in Egypt. They usually had two wheels and were drawn by two or more horses. The carriage itself was just a floor with a waist-high guard in front.

The Ethiopian treasurer was either a Jew or one who believed in the worship of the god of the Jews. He had come to Jerusalem to worship and was returning to his African land. As he traveled, he was reading aloud — as was the custom for reading at that time — from the prophecy of Isaiah. The chariot was evidently moving slowly, for Philip was able to run alongside it and ask the Ethiopian, "Do you understand what you are reading?" As it happened, he was reading the prophecy of Isaiah about the "sheep led to the slaughter," generally accepted as a prophecy of Christ.

Invited to step aboard the chariot, Philip was able to apply the prophecy to the good news of the coming of the Messiah. Impressed, the Ethiopian halted his vehicle at a desert well and asked Philip to baptize him. Such a well or oasis might have been dug out so that both beasts and people could drink from it. Usually the amount of water was scant, for it would evaporate quickly, but it was sufficient for both Philip and the Ethiopian to wade into it. Philip then disappeared, heading northward to Azotus (or Ashdod) while the Ethiopian continued his long homeward trip.

Ethiopia at that time was similar to the present land, although its borders may have included parts of what are now the Sudan and Egypt. There were black Jews living in Ethiopia who clung to the practices and beliefs of the ancient faith of Israel. They no longer held to all the orthodox rites, for this might have been impractical, but nevertheless they worshiped the God of Abraham and claimed a common ancestry with other Jews. Such black-skinned Jews still exist today. Ancient tradition holds that long before the time of Abraham, one of the three sons of Noah, named Ham, was cursed because he saw the nakedness and drunken disgrace of his father. The curse was that he became black-skinned. Ham's descendants bore names like Cush, Egypt, Ramah, Canaan, and Sheba, which leads to the belief that they peopled Africa and southern Asia. How some of these people later came into the Jewish fold is not clear, but various possibilities offer themselves. For example, maybe some of the Hebrews who were held captive in Egypt intermarried or escaped into other parts of Africa.

The established fact is that an Ethiopian eunuch, a trusted official in his government, a black man, a reader of the prophecy of Isaiah and a worshiper at the temple in Jerusalem, encountered Philip on a desert road near Gaza and was baptized in the name of Jesus.

An interesting corollary to this story is the fact that the Coptic Christian Church, now a small denomination centered in Egypt and Ethiopia, claims to trace its history back to this exact incident. To this day, the Copts look back to the time when one of their number visited Jerusalem and brought back with him to Ethiopia the knowledge of Jesus the Christ. Oddly enough, the Copts to this day circumcise male infants and observe some of the Mosaic dietary laws, an indication of their legendary status as a scattered Jewish sect.

The conversion of the eunuch is another finger of God reaching out to touch a particular individual, in this case leaping the barriers of race and nationality. Once again, it is the account of an individual being brought to Christ by the direct one-on-one contact with a disciple or evangelist. With billions of Christians in the world today, we cannot trace the course of the history of the church through each individual touched by the grace of God, but many examples support the belief that God's way to spread his kingdom is from one person to another person. There have been times when some despotic monarch became a Christian and issued a decree making every one of his subjects a Christian, but that is formality rather than conversion. God's kingdom reaches out to individuals one by one, and not en masse.

Here are two small incidents — the fingers of the dawn of Christianity stretching out, first to Simon in Samaria and then to the black man on the road to Gaza. Probably at some much later date, Philip recounted them to Luke, who preserved them for us in this fascinating manner. The events in Samaria were known to other Christians because they stirred a reaction in Jerusalem and encouraged Philip and John to leave the confines of Jerusalem to venture forth, at least for a few miles. But the incident on the desert must have been a matter known to Philip alone, for it figures no further in the accounts of the mission of the disciples.

Thoughts

(for personal reflection or group discussion)

1. Philip and Stephen are the best-known of the elders selected to assist the disciples. Their careers took different directions. Which one accomplished the most? Do you see parallels in such careers today?

2. Although Simon the Magician was "converted," he still craved additional powers and had to be scolded by Peter. What does "conversion" really mean? How is it related to baptism and confirmation?

3. Tradition holds that Simon of Cyrene, who carried the cross for Jesus, was a black man. The first person identified as a black who joined the followers of Jesus was an Ethiopian official whose name we do not know. What part did racial distinctions play in the spread of the Gospel then? What part do they play now?

Questions

1. What well-known converts to Christianity were won by Philip?

2. What is simony? Where did the name come from?

3. Where is Ethiopia? What was its connection to the early Christians?

4. Why was the baptism of the Ethiopian treasurer a major advance for Christianity?

5. What Old Testament prophecy led the Ethiopian to Christ?

Chapter 8

Brother Saul

Read Acts 9:1-31

Beginnings are always difficult, so the reports of the conversion of Simon the Sorcerer and the Ethiopian eunuch deserve the special mention that they have received. However, they pale in comparison with what comes next! After these two relatively minor incidents, we come to two tremendously big ones which have affected the whole church ever since. The first is the conversion of the fanatical persecutor, Saul, and the second is Peter's dramatic eye-opening to the fact that gentiles are included in God's redemptive grace.

To date these events correctly is difficult, but we know that they took place between five and ten years after the Resurrection. They were the first major break-outs from the Jewish cocoon, events which literally changed the world.

The rabbinical student Saul, who was almost psychotic in his bitter persecution of the harmless Christians, got an appointment from the High Priest to be the chief inquisitor for Jewish orthodoxy. He was authorized to search out any who followed the Way of Jesus and to deal with them as harshly as Jewish or Roman law would allow. His special assignment was to go to Damascus in Syria to ferret out people who were reported to belong to the Christian group there and to bring them back as prisoners to Jerusalem for trial before an ecclesiastical court.

A Man With Two Names

Before we go on, it may be well to establish what we know about Saul at this time. He was a man in his late twenties, a native of the city of Tarsus on the northeast coast of the Mediterranean in what is now Turkey. The region was then called Cilicia. Since Tarsus was a Roman city, he had been given two names, as was the custom. His Jewish name was Saul; his Roman name was Paul. A Jew born in a Roman city always received two names. One was his religious or ethnic name, the other was the civil name which would identify him as a citizen of Rome and would enable him to participate in commercial and social life without the stigma of seeming to be an outsider.

This custom isn't so strange, for it is still practiced in our times. In the Roman Catholic Church, for example, a child often has a given name which may be completely secular. At baptism, however, a ''religious'' name is added, often the name of a saint, in order to establish the child's Christian heritage. Even people moving from one nation or culture to another often adapt their names to the new environment. A boy born in Germany might be named Johannes, but when that child emigrates to America he is likely to call himself John simply in order to avoid the implication that he is a foreigner.

So Saul had two names and that's the whole meaning of the difference between Saul and Paul. You'll notice that in Acts, when Saul/Paul is among Jews he is designated as Saul but when among gentiles he's called Paul. To Romans, the name Paul would give him added stature for it would hide his ethnic relationship to the Jews, who were not usually well regarded in Roman communities.

Saul/Paul was a devout Jew, who came down to Jerusalem to complete his studies of Judaism with the aim of becoming a rabbi or teacher. He must have been a good student, for his special tutor was the Rabbi Gamaliel, the leading rabbi of that time. A member of the Sanhedrin, Gamaliel was an influential jurist and was held in high honor by the people. His wisdom was evidenced in his handling of the first accusations made against the disciples (5:34-39) when he cautiously advised his colleagues to be careful about taking hasty action. ''Let the Christians alone,'' he advised. ''If their plan or undertaking is of men, it will fail; but if it is of God, you will not be able to overthrow them. You might even be found to be opposing God!''

Like many students, Saul did not take his teacher's sound advice as seriously as he should have. Saul was full of nervous energy. He was an activist and tended to side with those who advocated immediate and strenuous action, even when such action was needless. While Gamaliel urged restraint in the oppression of the Christians,

Saul was much more impetuous. He decided that it was part of his duty as a zealous Jew to wipe out the new sect which might threaten his nation: to take preventive action, so to speak. He was therefore found among those consenting to the murder of Stephen. Because the temple officials approved militant action against any sect that threatened their revenues, they gave Saul high marks for his performance. As Saul himself admits later in his letter to the Galatians, he was a belligerent defender of Judaism who had advanced beyond many others of his own age in his zeal to preserve the traditions of the fathers.

A Light and a Voice

Armed with authority to spread the persecution of Christians to other cities, Saul set out for Damascus. On the way, something dramatic happened to him which he himself was at a loss to explain. Addressing a crowd in Jerusalem some twenty years later, Saul said that on the road to Damascus in the bright glare of the noonday sun a great light shone around him and he fell to the ground. He then heard a voice saying, "Saul, Saul, why do you persecute me?" He answered, "Who are you, Lord?"

That answer alone might indicate that Saul was already stricken in conscience for what he was doing and was somewhat fearful of the consequences if Jesus was indeed what he claimed to be. As a student of Gamaliel, Saul may have caught his teacher's warning. He must also have been familiar with the stories about Jesus and his mighty works. Students must have discussed and debated the teachings of Jesus, just as theological students today learn about and discuss pagan religions and the threat they may pose to Christianity. A seminary course called "Apologetics" is intended to teach the defense of the faith against those who would attack it. Whatever the name for a similar course may have been in Gamaliel's school, it was likely that Saul had learned much from it.

Whatever the thoughts that coursed through Saul's mind at the moment, he heard the answer clearly: "I am Jesus of Nazareth whom you are persecuting."

Saul's emotional turmoil at this point left him dazed. He told the Jews at Jerusalem that the others who were with him saw the great light but did not hear the voice. Yet in 9:7 the account is exactly opposite. Luke writes that those with Saul heard the words but evidently did not react to the great burst of light as Saul had. Is this a conflict of Scripture? It hardly seems likely, since both stories occur in the writing of Luke, who was too good a journalist to be caught in this kind of contradiction. Could both accounts be correct, then?

The differences do not trouble me in the least, for this was such a strange event, like an earthquake or sudden explosion, that accounts of eyewitnesses may differ. People are so shaken and frightened that they cannot think clearly for a moment and in retrospect each one may have a different reaction to what happened. Luke's first account comes from sources unknown, probably a summation of reports that filtered back to Jerusalem. Paul's own words at a much later date reflect his own recollection of this event. Any happening that can knock a person to the ground and strike him blind can also shock him so much that clear remembrance is difficult.

The fact that Saul was stricken blind is no surprise, either. Saul had been blind all along. He had been spiritually blind. His eyes were not open. He did not recognize the presence of Jesus Christ. But he did not know that he was blind! So in order that he might become convinced of his spiritual blindness, he was compelled to suffer a short period of physical or hysterical blindness. It was not that his sight was destroyed; it was simply a case where he was forced to realize that he could not see. Three days later his physical sight returned, evidently as good as it had been before. And as a bonus he was also given the power of spiritual sight so that what had been hidden from his eyes before the incident was fully revealed.

It had taken Saul about one week to make the trip from Jerusalem to Damascus, walking over the hot desert roads. Since the way wound from one village to another and around the mountains of northern Palestine, the distance would have been more than 150 miles. Covering twenty-five miles a day, it meant that Saul perhaps for the first time in his hyperactive life had ample time to think over what he was doing. He may have wondered whether the mission upon which he had embarked was right or wrong. Any disciple of Gamaliel would have had his conscience pricked by such a question. And Saul had been present, listening, when Stephen was stoned to death while making a glorious and brave defense of his Savior. Stephen had died in pain and torture but with a cry of triumph on his lips and a word of forgiveness for those who were killing him. That event alone must have made some impression on Saul, who was now on his way to deliver more victims to a similar fate.

Then came those words on the desert road: "I am Jesus, whom you are persecuting." Saul's response was a normal, "What shall I do, Lord ?" Yet the turmoil in his soul must have been overwhelming. Friendly hands helped him rise from the dust of the road and led him into Damascus. For three days he was in darkness, unable to see, and he spent the time in a total fast, neither eating nor drinking.

During this period, Saul was praying fervently. Certainly he was praying for a return of his vision, but he also must have been pleading for some explanation of the meaning of his experience.

Ananias, Reluctant Helper

After three days, a man named Ananias was sent to bring him a message. Ananias must have been one of the Christians who fled from Jerusalem because of persecution, for only in that way would he have known about Saul and the fact that Saul had authority from the high priests to seize and bind those who called on the name of Jesus. Naturally, Ananias was not happy about being chosen as a messenger to Saul. He was reluctant to go. The Bible is full of people who are called to a task by God but who undertake it only with great unwillingness, if at all. Moses was such a person; he fled and had to be convinced by a burning bush. Jonah was such a person; he fled to the farthest city to escape from the mission God had designated for him. Every minister in the church meets up with such reluctant people. Ask them to do something for their Lord and they can come up with a thousand excuses. "Somebody else is better equipped for this than I am . . . I'm too busy . . . I don't want to be involved . . ." Jesus even told a parable about those invited to the Gospel feast who were reluctant to come and instead made excuses.

So this Ananias, who must not be confused with the Ananias at Jerusalem who had attempted to deceive the disciples, cited the danger of dealing with Saul, who had done so much evil. He tried to get out of the mission, but could not. God had chosen him for a purpose and there's no escape from such a choice. Incidentally, this visit to Saul marks the only time we read or hear of this Ananias.

Ananias finally gave in and went with halting steps to the house of Judas on the street called Straight. Such a street still exists in Damascus. At Saul's time it was probably the Darb el-Moskatim, a street which runs through Damascus from east to west. Ananias found his fears unfounded. By the time he reached him, Saul had become a changed man. His three days of darkness had brought about a radical reversal in his thinking. Perhaps he identified himself with the three days Jesus had spent in the darkness of the tomb between death and resurrection, for the old Saul had died and a new one was ready to rise up. As God had said to Ananias, Saul had been made into a "chosen instrument of the Lord."

Despite his natural reluctance, Ananias showed a spirit of courage in going to Paul and a wonderful spirit of conciliation by addressing him as "Brother Saul." Ananias had accepted God's revelation that the former persecutor had now become a vessel chosen for a special purpose, like some prophets of old. As Ananias laid his hands on Saul, "something like scales" fell from Saul's eyes and he regained his sight. Saul was then baptized, presumably by Ananias. Perhaps much more was said and done, but we know only these few facts.

The Plot Against Saul

For several days Saul stayed at Damascus with the disciples of Jesus who were there. He even ventured into the synagogues and testified to Jesus, causing great confusion and perplexity. Saul obviously had great aggressiveness or nerve or "chutzpah" or whatever it may be called. He did not wait for a period of cooling off or for some sign of acceptance, but plunged right ahead as if he were the chief of the disciples! It's no wonder that the Jews at Damascus were confounded. Was Saul a double agent? Hadn't he come from Jerusalem with letters denouncing the Christians and entitling him to seize and persecute them? Now he had joined their ranks and presumed to be their spokesman. Small wonder that they stood for this only a little while before they began to plot to kill Saul. They regarded him as a dangerous double-dealer. Anyone who could not be trusted to carry out a mission for the high priests was not welcome in their synagogue to spread what they regarded to be false teaching. It was typical of the intrigue of those days and those people that they plotted to get rid of Saul by fair means or foul.

Figuring that Saul would soon leave the city, they laid a trap for him. They set watch at the city gates day and night waiting for him to make a move. Then they planned to catch him outside the city and to kill him. Evidently this would be done with full knowledge of the authorities, because Saul later writes that at Damascus, "the governor under King Aretas guarded the city in order to seize me, but I was let down in a basket through a window in the wall and escaped outside.''

Damascus at this time was under the jurisdiction of Aretas IV, king of Nabatea, an area southeast of Palestine. Aretas and Herod Antipas were rivals for authority in the Roman-ruled area along the eastern Mediterranean. It is possible that the Romans left the control of the outlying sections to the local kings, for there is no mention of Roman intervention in this matter even though Saul speaks of a "governor." Like all people whose territory is occupied by a foreign power, the Jews tried in every possible way to squirm out from under the Roman fist. Whenever they could take advantage of some incident without deliberately violating the restrictions laid down by Rome, they promptly did so. It looks therefore as if Aretas was playing along with the religious leaders of Damascus in order to cement his claim to dominance in the region, thereby undercutting Herod Antipas as well as the Romans.

In any event, Saul got out of the city by being let down through a window in the city wall under cover of darkness. Later Saul wrote to the Corinthians listing this as one of his sufferings as an apostle.

There are several versions of what happened after Saul's conversion. As a reporter, Luke had to sift through many stories told him by different people. In one of his letters, Saul indicates that after his conversion he had spent much time in the desert before returning to Damascus to preach. He writes to the Galatians, "I did not confer with flesh and blood, nor did I go up to Jerusalem to those who were apostles before me, but I went away into Arabia; and again I returned to Damascus.''

To reconstruct the events on a firm time schedule is therefore difficult. In spite of what he wrote to the Galatians, it seems likely that after his conversion experience, Saul spent some time at Damascus. If three years had passed before Saul came back to preach, the Damascene Jews would not have been so perplexed by the conversion. It seems more likely that he escaped from Damascus as reported and then spent a period of time in seclusion, perhaps in the Arabian desert. Giving added support to this order of events is the fact that if King Aretas was out to get him, collaborating with the high priests, it would scarcely have made sense for Saul to head straight to Jerusalem where an openly hostile reception awaited him. He would do better to hide out for a time.

When Saul finally did get to Jerusalem, even if it was three years later, his reputation was still strong enough to terrify the disciples. They wanted nothing to do with him. And we can't blame them.

The disciples said, "This is the fellow who was persecuting the church. Now he has come back saying that he wants to be a disciple and that he has a special order from God entitling him to be the chosen instrument to carry the name of Jesus to gentiles and kings and sons of Israel? Nothing doing!" The leaders of the Jerusalem church felt that Saul needed a period of probation. Even though he professed to be a believer in Jesus, he was too volatile and undependable to be allowed into the inner circle.

Barnabas to the Rescue

Now a new name, Barnabas, crops up. It was Barnabas who befriended Saul and persuaded the disciples to accept him. Barnabas (4:36) had been given that name, which means "Son of Encouragement," by the disciples. Formerly named Joseph, he was a Levite, a native of Cyprus, who had sold his property and become a liberal contributor to the church. Now Barnabas appears to be taking a leading position among the disciples. Apostles like Peter and John and others who are better known seem now to be lacking leadership, while a lay member of the congregation, Barnabas, makes the next great move for the advancement of the work of the church. We should have more churches named for Saint Barnabas! While the apostles held aloof, Barnabas evidently had long conversations with Saul. He discussed Saul with others and came to the conclusion that Saul's conversion was valid. So he brought Saul to the other apostles and explained to them what he had discovered about his conversion and what he believed. Despite their respect for Barnabas, the other apostles never really accepted Saul. They allowed Saul to mingle with the other members of the group, but they still held him at a distance. They said, "He does not deserve to be in with the rest of us because of his record."

This kind of response is still common among us. There is supposed to be great joy in heaven over a sinner who repents, but Christian congregations do not often echo that joy. If someone in the community or congregation does some terrible thing or commits some grievous sin, but then repents and asks forgiveness and desires to be restored to the fold, he may be allowed to come back but finds himself snubbed or treated coldly. Such a person is usually watched carefully so that we can be certain he will not resume his wicked ways. This is surely the case when someone has served a prison sentence and comes out "reformed" and eager to re-enter society. As soon as it is mentioned that the person was once in prison, coolness and reserve develops. This is not a good thing nor a proper Christian attitude, but it is human nature. "We can't forget what he did," people say.

So it was with the disciples. They let Saul into the group, but they refused to be intimate with him. With his usual self-assurance, Saul did not seem to care. He went in and out among them and preached boldly in the name of the Lord. Then he even took on the Hellenists, the crowd that had put Stephen to death. These people formed the Synagogue of the Freedmen and were evidently the most belligerent of the Jewish groups. These Hellenists evidently relished the challenge. "We got rid of Stephen, but now there's a new fly in the ointment. Let's get Saul, the turncoat." And so they sought to kill him.

When the disciples learned of this new threat to the peace of the church, they took Saul and escorted him to Caesarea, where they put him on a ship and sent him off to Tarsus, his native city. We don't know what explanation they gave him, for Saul was hardly the type of person to take this sort of exile without putting up a fight, but they might have pointed out that the church had enjoyed peace for three years while Saul was in the desert, and while they loved him and all that, now that he was back things were going from bad to worse and for the church's sake wouldn't it be a good idea if he took a little vacation and went home to see his folks in Tarsus? Whatever they said, they obviously wanted to get rid of Saul. He was a disturber and he threatened to bring on new persecutions. He had to be gotten out of the way.

Sometimes there is no alternative to this kind of action. Even in a congregation there can be well-meaning but bumbling persons who seem to cause trouble by what they do or say. Sometimes there is no solution except to get them out of the way, for the sake of the peace of the rest of the community. Saul seemed to have an exceptional faculty for stirring up trouble. Wherever he went, sooner or later he caused a disturbance and was chased away!

The threat of trouble that hung over the Jerusalem church appears to have been dissolved as soon as Saul was sent off. In 9:31

we read what happened: "So the church throughout all Judea and Galilee and Samaria had peace and was built up." The "so" is revealing. Once Saul had been sent off, peace returned! The church grew and maybe Saul also grew. He now had a period of some two or three years to be by himself, away from the main body of the disciples, perhaps to mature in faith and to realize the need for developing peace and harmony in a Christian community rather than an abrasive and aggressive insistence on one's own way. In this case he was not unlike others whom we may have encountered along the way. Even though they are right and even though they preach the truth, we somehow become annoyed with them because they are so self-assured and self-righteous in their manner. That was the case with the early Paul!

But the conversion of Saul was a great breakthrough in the history of this band of followers of the Way, for by his conversion their arch enemy had not only been silenced but had actually been won over and made into an ally. It was a milestone in Christian history, too, for when he matured and grew in love and understanding, the rich talent and boundless energy of Saul brought the message of Jesus to the whole gentile world.

Thoughts

(for personal reflection or group discussion)

1. Is it true that converts often become the most vigorous advocates of a cause? Someone who has given up smoking, for example, is likely to be aggressive in urging others to give it up also. And some of the most effective Christian missionaries have come from those who once actively opposed Christ. Why?

2. "They have eyes, but see not," Jeremiah 5:21 says of those who turn away from God. Evidently there are different kinds of blindness. How can we find our personal "blind spots"? Do we possess "spiritual sight"?

3. Suppose someone who had a long criminal record came into your congregation and asked to be accepted as a member. How would he be received? Or how would one who came from a vastly different social or ethnic background be received? Would some (or all) members have reservations about being too friendly?

Questions

1. How did Saul, a Jew, get the name of Paul?

2. What was Saul's educational background?

3. Why was Saul going to Damascus? What actually happened on the Damascus Road?

4. Why was Ananias fearful of visiting Saul at the house of Judas?

5. Why were both Damascus Jews and Christians perplexed by Saul's preaching?

6. What happened in the churches in "Judea and Galilee and Samaria" after Saul was bundled off to Tarsus?

Chapter 9

Conversion of a Soldier

Read Acts 9:32—11:30

With the departure of Saul, the scene shifts and the spotlight is once again on Peter, who emerges from time to time as the leader of the disciples. Peter was always their highly-respected anchor man, stalwart and dependable, although others were more brilliant and occasionally took command. Peter was always in the midst of things, however. He had faced persecution like the others and had matured in faith, gaining greater understanding of the power that accrued to those who relied confidently on the presence and the help of Jesus. You might call him a born-again Simon Peter, for he had developed the kind of confidence that is based on accomplishment rather than bravado.

When the disciples spread out from Jerusalem, Peter and John had been sent to confirm the work being done in Samaria. Later, Peter moved about among the towns of Judea, coming to Lydda, a village about twenty-five miles northwest of Jerusalem. The most traveled road from Jerusalem to Lydda led through Emmaus and then on to Joppa (modern Tel Aviv) on the seacoast. Air travelers to Israel today usually arrive and leave from Lod Airport. Lod is the modern name for Lydda. It's now an industrial city, site of Israel's aircraft factories. Like many places in the Holy Land, it has an ancient history buried under tons of rubble, for it was destroyed and rebuilt many times. The city was once a Palestinian stronghold, but the Palestinians fled after the establishment of the nation of Israel in 1948.

The Christian community in Lydda must have been large. After Peter healed a paralytic named Aeneas, who was either Greek or who had a Greek name, "all the residents" of Lydda and the surrounding Plain of Sharon "turned to the Lord." The healing of Aeneas, of whom we hear nothing more, was a major event.

Tabitha a.k.a. Dorcas

Peter then moved on to a more famous city, Joppa (or Jaffa). Located on the coast, Joppa was an important port from earliest times right up to World War II. It was the place where Jonah had boarded a ship in his effort to escape doing God's will. With ships from distant places stopping at Joppa, it was cosmopolitan even in the time of the disciples. This mixture of people is indicated by the two names of the woman disciple, Tabitha (Aramaic) and Dorcas (Greek). Probably she was a Greek-born Jew. Today her Greek name, Dorcas, is synonymous with one who does good works of charity and kindness, for such was her reputation. Peter was still at Lydda when Dorcas fell sick and died. Her body was prepared for burial, but was not immediately put into the tomb but instead was placed in an upper room while messengers were hastily sent to Peter, asking him to come without delay. Why would they have done such a thing? Dorcas was already dead and Peter was at least a two-hour journey distant. Perhaps they knew that Lazarus was dead when Jesus had been summoned to him.

Whatever the reason, Peter rose and went with them at once. He apparently disregarded the evidence of her death. Chasing the mourners out of the house, he prayed and called to her, "Tabitha, arise!" She opened her eyes and sat up. Peter then took her by the hand and called in the "saints and widows." One can only imagine the shrieks and shouts and excitement that followed! No wonder the news of the event traveled like wildfire up and down the coast.

Peter, Simon, and Cornelius

With each incident related in this section of *Acts*, the Gospel reaches out a little further. Not only were devout Jews hearing the word and experiencing the power of Christ, but Samaritans were being brought into the fold. In Joppa the circle widened a little more, for Peter stayed at the home of Simon, a tanner. This in itself was a remarkable stride forward. A tanner was one whose trade was to strip the hide from dead animals and work it into leather, a pursuit considered unclean under Jewish law. Simon would therefore not have been welcomed into the house of a Pharisee nor would he have been permitted to enter the temple at Jerusalem. If he was a Jew — and there is no reason to question this — he was nevertheless a sort of outcast. For Peter to stay under his roof was a sign that Peter fully accepted that the mission of the disciples was to all the world. The next incident strengthens this belief.

The next step in the outreach of the disciples brought them to Caesarea, a Roman city about thirty miles north of Joppa on the Mediterranean shore. Two Roman cities are to figure prominently in the next advance of the Gospel — Caesarea and Antioch. The center of action is stretching out farther from Jerusalem.

The catalyst at Caesarea was Cornelius, a Roman centurion who commanded the legion known as the Italian Cohort. Roman history identifies this as a crack Italian regiment, *Cohors II, Italica Civium Romanorum*. As the centurion of this regiment, Cornelius commanded one hundred men. Centurions were soldiers who had risen through the ranks and who had shown exceptional courage and reliability. Centurions reported directly to a tribune, who was usually a person of a noble family who combined his military and civic duties and who in this case might be a sort of military governor in an occupied land like Palestine.

Cornelius held a high rank in the military and was also a devout man who gave alms liberally and who prayed constantly to God. He was a most unusual soldier, one might say! Perhaps he had been stationed in Palestine for a long time, because he seems to have embraced some Jewish customs. He was a man of some distinction and a trusted leader, not the sort of person given to wild dreams and strange ideas. Yet Cornelius saw an angel in a dream and the angel instructed him to send for Peter, a Jewish fisherman who happened to be at nearby Joppa. Cornelius was not disobedient to the heavenly vision, just as Paul later confessed that he had obeyed the vision which came to him. So Cornelius sent two servants, evidently civilians, and a trusted soldier to bring Peter to him.

"Unclean" Redefined

At the same time, Peter was having an unusual dream which repeated itself three times. It happened in the middle of the day, at high noon, as Peter was on the sunny rooftop praying. In a sort of trance, Peter saw a great sheet let down to earth, and in it were all kinds of animals and reptiles and birds. The sheet might very well have been something like the leather awning which hung over the roof. With it came a voice saying, "Rise, Peter, kill and eat." The text says that Peter was hungry, so perhaps it was natural that he should dream of eating, but surely he would never dream of eating such an assortment of food. Peter rejected the voice in the dream, protesting that he had never eaten anything common or unclean and was not about to do such a thing at this time. According to Leviticus, the Jews were permitted to eat only certain kinds of meat, such as that which came from an animal with cloven hoofs, like a horse or cow. These were animals which ate only grass and herbs, as contrasted with other animals that fed on carrion or flesh. But here Peter was being urged to eat all kinds of flesh, including reptiles which were absolutely off limits for Jews, as indeed they are for most of us! Then the voice added a reprimand: "What God has cleansed, you must not call common!"

What would you make of a dream like that, repeated three times? Peter must have been shaken and troubled by the vision. While he was still wondering and perplexed, the explanation came. The dream had nothing to do with cuisine or menus. It had deeper implications. It was not an order to break the Jewish dietary law, but rather an eye-opener about God's love for all people. For even while Peter was pondering the strange revelation, news came that three men were knocking on the door of Simon's house and asking to see Peter. They were the emissaries from the Roman centurion, Cornelius. They asked Peter to come to the house of the gentile, Cornelius, so the centurion might hear what he had to say.

Going into the house of a gentile was strictly forbidden for Jews. Remember that when Jesus was on trial before Pilate, Pilate came out on the porch of his house so that Jesus, a Jew, might not be "defiled" by going into a gentile's house. But now Peter was being asked to come to the house of a gentile — and not just any gentile, but an important Roman officer. Peter's first reaction must have been that he would break Jewish law by going into such a house. But wasn't that what the thrice-repeated dream was all about?

Simon the Tanner had to expand his hospitality that night to accommodate the three messengers from the centurion, but by the next morning Peter had made up his mind. He went with the three, taking along also some disciples from the church at Joppa. When the group entered the house of the centurion, the Roman soldier fell down at Peter's feet. Peter raised him up, saying, "Stand up; I too am a man." By this time Peter had grasped the full meaning of his vision. It had been a message to teach him that all that God has created is good and that nothing in God's creation is to be despised or scorned. Peter therefore said nothing about food, but rather told Cornelius, "God has shown me that I should not call any man common, or unclean." His revelation was not about the birds or reptiles or animals, but rather about the unity of humankind.

Cornelius then explained to Peter that he, too, had seen a vision telling him to send for Peter. Before Peter had a chance to comment on the coincidence, Cornelius said, "Now therefore we are all here present in the sight of God, to hear all that you have been commanded by the Lord." How could a gentile say this? Peter must have wondered, but he responded with a sermon about the presence of Jesus Christ, how he was sent by God to live and die so that people might be saved, how he was rejected by his own people and suffered at their hands, only to rise again from the dead. Even as he was saying these things, Peter's mind must have been in a whirl wondering what would come next. Suppose Cornelius professed to believe and asked to be baptized? Dare he go so far as to accept him into the community of the saved? Cornelius was a gentile, not a Jew. Dare Peter overstep the previous limits so far as to receive him?

The Holy Spirit's Entry

But Peter never had to answer his own questionings. They were answered for him. While Peter was still preaching, the Holy Spirit fell on all who heard his words. The believers among the circumcised — that is, the Jewish Christians who had come with Peter — were amazed because the Spirit fell not only on them but also on the gentiles, with the result that all of them spoke in tongues and extolled God. When this happened, Peter turned to the Jews who had come with him and asked, "Can anyone forbid these people to be baptized, for they have received the Holy Spirit just as we have?"

Maybe this was a little like that point in the traditional marriage service where the minister asks, "Can anyone show just cause why this man and this woman should not be joined together in Holy Matrimony? If so, let him now speak or forever hold his peace." Peter was asking almost the same question, though under different circumstances. "Can I be forbidden from baptizing these people who have just received the power of the Holy Spirit?" Just as in the wedding service nobody is likely to speak up at this point, so nobody spoke up to interfere with what Peter had already determined to do. He commanded them to be baptized in the name of Jesus Christ!

For the first time, the Christian faith broke through ethnic barriers and into the heart of a gentile, a non-Jew, Cornelius. He and all his household were received into the Christian fold. While the baptism of a non-circumcised person violated the current practice of the Christian community, Peter by the power of the Holy Spirit made the decision to take them into the church. As we learn later, the same thing was being done elsewhere. But Peter had no way of knowing that, so he pioneered independently and entirely on his own. It was a daring leap in faith for Peter and for us.

Peter had some further hurdles to jump, however. The apostles and brethren who were in Judea heard about what had happened, so when Peter went back to Jerusalem they were lying in wait for him. The "circumcision party" reprimanded him, demanding to know why Peter had gone to the house of gentiles and eaten with them. Oddly enough, their slavish adherence to the law crops up first of all in this criticism. They didn't complain because Peter had actually baptized these people; they were more concerned about the Levitical law which forbade eating with gentiles! Naturally, the law said nothing about baptizing them.

The censure of Peter is the first inkling that there were separate factions within the Christian community even at that time. There was one "party" which held that the Christian faith was exclusively for Jews, that it was a Jewish sect without a mandate to reach out to the rest of the world. When Peter had explained his vision and the subsequent outpouring of the Spirit at the centurion's house, this opposition group was silenced. They were not convinced, however; they were only silenced for the moment. This is important to note because the selfsame arguments and the same resistance keeps cropping up again and again. A powerful clique held to the belief that to be a Christian one must first become a Jew. They could simply not rise enough above their heritage to see that God's kingdom extends beyond the borders of race and ethnic background. For the moment they accepted Peter's word and rejoiced that God had granted repentance to some gentiles, but it was only a grudging admission.

But the breakthrough was beyond reversal. The Gospel had exploded beyond the barriers of circumcision and ethnic heritage and constricting laws. The Word was no longer bound by the shackles of Jewish feelings of divine election. The Good News was on its way out into the world.

Peter's experience at Caesarea was being matched elsewhere. Those who had been scattered because of persecution traveled to distant places like Phoenicia, Cyprus and Antioch, well outside the boundaries of the Jewish nation, witnessing to all who would listen. A stirring event took place at Antioch when new converts from Cyprus and Cyrene came and preached the message of Jesus to Greeks as well as to Jews. A great number of those who heard turned to the Lord.

Rapid Growth at Antioch

When news of this came to Jerusalem, where the church was still reeling under the impact of Peter's report about the conversion of the Roman soldier Cornelius, there was both rejoicing and dismay. The Jerusalem church decided at once to send Barnabas up to Antioch to investigate what was going on. He found that a "large company" was added to the Lord, a congregation of gentiles — not just a single convert, but a large company! Barnabas was delighted and exhorted all of them to remain faithful and steadfast. Antioch, incidentally, was the third largest city in the Roman Empire, with a population of 600,000. It was the capital of Syria and was sometimes called the "Oriental Rome." It had much trade, a university, good roads and a full measure of Roman frivolity. A church established among these people would have much visibility and prestige. Here at Antioch the disciples were for the first time called Christians.

While at Antioch, it was quite natural for Barnabas to travel the relatively short distance to Tarsus to look for Saul. Barnabas had been the one who befriended Saul several years earlier and who had brought him into the inner circle of the disciples. Although Tarsus was also a good-sized city, Barnabas found Saul and brought him back to Antioch. We never learn what happened to Saul during his years at Tarsus, but obviously he had matured and developed both in his Christian faith and in his ability to deal with people.

For one whole year that happy congregation at Antioch had Barnabas as its senior pastor and Saul as his assistant. Their ministry resulted in the development of a strong and active congregation. When news reached Antioch about a famine in the land of Judea, causing great hardship among the members of the Christian community, the prosperous people of Antioch felt that they needed to express their love by sending help. They gave food and money willingly and gladly, commissioning Barnabas and Saul to bring these relief goods to Jerusalem. The gifts of the gentile Christians at Antioch thus went to sustain the Jewish Christians of Jerusalem, who had once thought themselves the only ones who were worthy to follow Christ. The date was about A.D. 46.

Thoughts

(for personal reflection or group discussion)

1. Dreams and their interpretation play an important role in the Bible, from the time when Joseph won fame in Egypt by interpreting Pharaoh's dream, right through to Peter and Paul. Is this superstition? How can a Christian evaluate dreams? Have you ever had dreams that meaningfully changed your life?

2. Several times we read that a whole household is converted and baptized. In later church history, there are times when the conversion of a king or prince meant that a whole realm was swept into the church. Are mass conversions really effective or must each individual receive Christ personally?

3. "Inclusiveness" is a term we apply to our church today. How inclusive do we really want to be? Isn't it likely that by including some people we may exclude others? How do we decide which is more important?

Questions

1. What foods are forbidden under Jewish dietary law?

2. How was Peter received at Jerusalem after he had baptized gentiles?

3. What did Barnabas find when he arrived at Antioch?

4. How was Saul brought back into the Christian ministry?

5. Where did the name "Christian" first come into use?

Chapter 10

Conflict with a King

Read Acts 12:1-24

While the church at Antioch grew and prospered, difficult times had come to the Christian community at Jerusalem. Not only was there famine and hardship in the land, but a new spate of persecution developed. Seeking to win favor with the Pharisees, King Herod Agrippa I responded to their urging that he crack down on dissident sects. Among the first victims were some of the leaders of the Christians. James, the son of Zebedee and the brother of John, was murdered by soldiers and Peter was arrested and thrown into prison. By a miraculous intervention, Peter was released from jail in the darkness of midnight.

Even in this tragic setting, Luke's account finds room for a lighter touch. The frightened disciples had gathered behind locked doors at the home of Mary, the mother of John Mark. With James lying dead and Peter supposedly in prison, they had come together for prayer and for mutual protection. Once freed from prison, the fugitive Peter hastened through the dark streets of the city to seek refuge in Mary's house, doubtless moving as swiftly and silently as possible with many a glance over his shoulder to make sure the soldiers were not pursuing him. When he knocked at the door of Mary's house, just one step away from the danger of the streets, a maid answered. Probably she was wise enough to ask before opening the door, "Who is it ?" When Peter answered, "It is I, Peter," she recognized his voice and in her excitement did not open the door but rather ran back to the praying assembly and said, "Peter is at the gate!" They said to her, "You are out of your mind." Evidently they argued for several minutes before they heard the continued knocking at the door and finally opened it so Peter could come in!

The death of kings and jailbreaks are the stuff of which news is made. Such exciting events would surely be played up in the newspapers.

From the Jerusalem *Post*,
April 10, A.D. 44

Dangerous Prisoner Escapes; Prison Guards To Be Executed

Following a mysterious jailbreak in which a dangerous political prisoner escaped, King Herod Agrippa I yesterday ordered six prison guards to be put to death. "The circumstances surrounding the disappearance of the radical Jew, Peter of Galilee, indicate conspiracy," our gracious monarch said in pronouncing sentence.

Evidence at the brief trial held in the king's chambers indicated that Peter had been chained hand and foot and was guarded by two soldiers. Four other soldiers were on duty at the prison door.

"No one could have gotten out of jail under these circumstances without the connivance or help of some or all the guards," royal prosecutor Schlomo said. He added mockingly, "That is, unless a big bird or a superman swooped down and carried him away." His remark applied to testimony given by the guards at the prison door, who claimed that a bright light had shone around them and blinded them just before the prisoner vanished.

Peter was arrested three weeks ago as part of our gracious monarch's plan to wipe out the radical Nazarene sect which claims to be followers of a criminal named Jesus, who was crucified about twelve years ago. The sect clings to the belief that Jesus arose from the dead and still abides with them. Earlier this month, after charges had been filed against him by the Pharisee party, James ben Zebedee, one of their leaders was executed.

According to the Galilee Poll, a large majority of the Pharisees and a smaller majority among the Sadducees favor the complete extermination of all such radical sects. The government policy was formulated in response to this expression of public opinion.

Evidence at the trial indicated that some strange circumstances may have surrounded the prison break. The chains which bound Peter were still tightly locked, indicating according to the prosecutor that accomplices of the prisoner must have possessed keys to unlock the chains from his hands and feet and then to lock them again. The iron gate to the prison was also locked. The key to this gate, however, was kept by the

Captain of the Guard and was not out of his possession during the night. There was no evidence of forcible tampering with the gate's lock. "He might have been hoisted over the wall," the captain suggested.

The escape of this important prisoner puts a crimp into King Herod's goal of eliminating the Nazarene sect completely. Charges are now being formulated against other members of the group who are known to be in Jerusalem, but large nests of these radicals are said to exist at Damascus, Cyprus and Antioch, as well as in some Judean towns.

Police yesterday searched all the known hangouts of the Jesus sect, but to no avail. A group of women that had gathered at the home of the widow Mary was taken into custody for questioning. Several of the women testified that they had seen spirits and angels, but they were dismissed as hysterical.

A watch was being kept throughout the city for James ben Joseph, said to be the brother of Jesus and the current leader of the sect. Sentries have been placed around Mary's house in case James attempts to contact any of the other followers of Jesus.

From the Rome *Tribune-Observer*
June 1, A.D. 44

Jewish King Dies Suddenly; Rift With Rome Is Avoided

Special to the Tribune-Observer

(Jerusalem, Judea) — King Herod Agrippa I died here this week after a brief illness, ending his three-year reign over this province. Agrippa, who was the grandson of King Herod the Great, had lived in Rome during his youth and was a close friend of former Emperor Caligula. He was thirty-four years old.

The sudden death of the king prevented a possible rift between Rome and the recently unified Kingdom of Judea, for Herod was reported to have recently proclaimed himself a god. Since our Noble Caesar, the Emperor Tiberius Claudius I, is the sole divine ruler in the empire, other kings are not permitted to claim divinity and Herod's position would have been untenable.

Herod's death occurred shortly after a delegation from Tyre and Sidon in Samaria came to this city to sue for peace and to acknowledge Herod's rule over the northern territories. The delegation also hoped to arrange for shipments of grain to be made to their area, which has been suffering famine. After Herod addressed the delegation at great length, outlining his noble heritage and proclaiming that the kingdom and power of David and Solomon were now held by him, the crowd shouted, "The voice of a god!" Herod accepted this homage, leading to the belief that he would soon announce his divinity.

As Herod was receiving the acclaim of the crowd, an owl perched on a rope holding the royal canopy. Herod immediately turned and left the balcony. Chief Chamberlain Blasias said the king was stricken with abdominal pains shortly afterward and blamed the owl, which he regarded as an omen of doom.

Herod's death aroused mixed reactions throughout Judea. Conservative Jews mourned his loss, since he had been engaged in a systematic campaign to wipe out all deviate religious groups. Samaritans and Phoenicians, however, claimed that Herod had ruled by bloodbaths and torture and expressed the hope that future conditions would be better.

When word of Herod's death reached the imperial palace, Emperor Claudius decreed that the Judean kingdom be divided once again into four tetrarchies, as it was before Herod's accession. He named Cuspius Fadus as the new governor of the province of Palestine.

To these news reports we need only add two important notes. The first deals with the sense of relief that must have swept over the Christian community after Herod's death. Herod's three-year regime had been a time of terror and persecution, including not only the murder of James and the imprisonment of Peter, but constant harrassment and persecution by the Pharisees against the Christians, with the hearty support of the king. Herod's ambition to restore the eminence of the Jewish kingdom to the glories of David and Solomon's time would inevitably have led to armed clashes with Rome. This would have resulted in the destruction of the Jewish cities and the suppression of the Jewish people. This is exactly what happened in A.D. 70.

Christians therefore hailed Herod's death as divine punishment. Perhaps it was! After Herod died, "the word of God grew and multiplied." Barnabas and Saul, who presumably were at Jerusalem throughout this trying period in the life of the church, returned to

Antioch bringing with them a young disciple named John Mark.

The other interesting development that emerges during this incident is the identification of James, the brother of Jesus, as the leader of the Christian community at Jerusalem and therefore in effect the head of the entire Christian movement. This is borne out in 15:13, where James presides at a council meeting: in 21:18, where Paul is called in to confer with James and the other elders; and in Galatians 2:9, where the leaders of the church are listed as James, Cephas and John, with James named first. This would account for Peter's word after his escape from prison, to "tell this to James and the brethren." James is singled out because he was the leader.

But who was James? He was not one of the original twelve, nor was he one of those added as elders during the first years of the church. He gets his first mention in Matthew 13:55 when the people in Jesus' home town said of him, "Is not this the carpenter's son? Is not his mother called Mary? Are not his brothers James and Joseph and Simon and Judas?"

Assuming then that James was the brother of Jesus, he must have been well acquainted with the life and ministry of the Lord. He was surely closer to Mary than any of the others. Some time after the death and resurrection of Jesus, James became a believer. His mother would certainly have tried to convince him, even if other proofs were missing. But James was one who had seen the risen Jesus (1 Corinthians 15:7) and could not have remained outside of the fold after that personal revelation. And since James was probably with his mother in Jerusalem, he would have been involved in all the work of the church.

Some twelve years have passed since the resurrection and we need to remember that the number twelve had special meaning for the Jews. The disciples had been told to remain at Jerusalem, but without a definite time limit. Twelve years would have seemed to them as a proper length of time encompassed in such a command, since twelve is one of the "holy numbers" and indicates completeness. As the disciples left Jerusalem and scattered, the brother of the Lord would be an obvious choice to head the church. In a nation accustomed to royalty, James in a sense was a member of the "royal family." Later records indicate that James was a good pastor, a model of piety who exhorted people to put their faith into action by loving and sharing with one another. He also took the lead in conciliating disputes, as we shall see when he brings about the agreement that gentile Christians need not be burdened with the Jewish law. Probably he was also the author of the epistle that bears the name of James. Tradition says that he was the first "bishop" of Jerusalem, and that he was stoned to death about A.D. 62, during one of the frequent persecutions of the Jerusalem church by the fanatical Jewish religious leaders.

Thoughts

(for personal reflection or group discussion)

1. The Pharisees were the strictest of the Jews in their observance of the Law, even in its minor points. Yet Jesus said they were cold, stiff-necked and unmerciful. Sometimes very pious people today show the same absence of love and tolerance. Where should we draw the line between *law* and *love*?

2. Herod's sudden death saved the Christians from further persecution. Does God strike down enemies of his people by supernatural means? If so, how did Hitler, Hirohito and the Ayatollah escape?

3. Herod Agrippa I was probably the least qualified of all the Herod "family" to rule Israel. He was small-minded, petty and covetous, yet he claimed special honor and homage. Petty leaders often do this even when they are only president of the PTA or mayors of small towns! How can we make sure not to think of ourselves more highly than we ought to think?

Questions

1. Why was Peter cast into prison? How did he get out?

2. Why did the Christians rejoice over the death of Herod?

3. Is it ever proper for Christians to rejoice over the death of their enemies?

4. Assemble all the facts about James. Why did Herod kill him?

5. After the death of James the son of Zebedee, another James holds a prominent place in the Christian community. Who was the other James?

Chapter 11

Sorting Out the Herods

This may be as good a place as any to sort out the kings named Herod, who figure again and again in the pages of the New Testament. The preceding news item introduces one of these Herods and then removes him abruptly. He was not long on the New Testament scene, but other Herods crop up at climactic times throughout the narrative.

When Jesus was an infant in Bethlehem, it was a King Herod who killed all male children in an attempt to eradicate this newcomer whom he considered a threat to his throne. Having been warned in a dream, Mary and Joseph fled with the infant Jesus to Egypt and thus escaped. Later, John the Baptizer was beheaded by a King Herod, whom Jesus disdainfully referred to as "that fox." During his trial, Jesus was sent by Pontius Pilate to a King Herod who happened to be in Jerusalem. Late in Paul's career he appeared before a King Herod Agrippa who listened intently to Paul's preaching.

Herod Antipater

Clearly these Herods were not one and the same. They represented a line of monarchs, all with similar names but with highly dissimilar characters. Because of the mixed-up family situation whereby a king might have several wives plus concubines, we are not even sure of the exact ancestry of the family. The dynasty began about 65 B.C. with an Edomite named Antipater, who gained a strong foothold in Palestine by allying himself with the Roman expeditionary forces. His son, also named Antipater, was made ruler of Palestine by Julius Caesar. When Antipater died, he gave the land to his sons, Phasael and Herod. Phasael was killed by a Parthian uprising, but Herod survived and fled to Rome, where he was given training in government affairs and military matters.

"Herod The Great"

Herod made a good impression on Marc Antony, who headed the government after the murder of Julius Caesar, and was commissioned in 39 B.C. as the "king of Judea" with the mandate to recapture the Middle East for the Romans. Supplied with adequate provisions and an able army, Herod accomplished this task in less than three years, bringing under his control the lands of Galilee, Judea and Samaria and making them provinces of Rome. He did his job so well that he earned the title of "Herod the Great." He reigned about thirty-four years. Among his accomplishments was the building of the city of Caesarea on the shore of the Mediterranean. Since the area had no good port city, Caesarea was an important addition as a commercial center and a place of embarkation for ships and troops shuttling between Rome and Palestine. Herod further cemented his relationships with the Romans after Augustus Caesar was placed on the throne by building a temple to Augustus in Samaria.

A temple built to honor a Roman god-emperor was not pleasing to the Jews, who disliked Herod anyway because of his Edomite background. Herod therefore placated them by building a fine Jewish temple at Jerusalem. Herod was a practical politician! The edifice at Jerusalem was known as Herod's Temple and it was to this magnificent new temple that Jesus came when he was twelve years old.

Herod was a complex personality, however, and some even thought him insane. He had ten wives. His cruelties were legendary. For example, his murder of the infants at Bethlehem was quite in keeping with his character, since he had previously killed at least three of his own sons.

Herod Antipas

Herod the Great died about 2 B.C., according to our reckoning. He was succeeded by three of his sons. His realm was divided between Archelaus, Herod Antipas and Philip. Archelaus, who ruled Judea, had evidently inherited his father's ruthlessness but not his father's diplomacy. He vexed the Jews so much that there were constant rebellions and finally he was banished by Rome at the demand of the Jews. Herod Antipas then assumed the rule over Judea as well as Galilee, clinging to his crown for about forty years. He was the king who beheaded John the Baptizer and who was in office during the ministry of Jesus. He was the Herod to whom Jesus was sent by Pilate, and his woeful ignorance of spiritual affairs was clearly shown by his handling of the interview with Jesus. Herod was baffled by Jesus and made no effort to understand him. He asked Jesus to perform a miracle for him, as if he were dealing with a magician or trickster. Jesus showed his scorn for this Herod by refusing even to speak to him.

Herod Agrippa I

When Herod Antipas died, he was succeeded by his nephew, Herod Agrippa I, in A.D. 41. Herod Agrippa reigned only three years. Striving to win favor with the Jews, he persecuted the Christians. He put James to death and when he saw that this pleased the Jews, he arrested Peter. The miserable death of Herod Agrippa I could scarcely have caused much mourning in the land, certainly not among the Christians. While the biblical account indicates that Herod died instantly, this may have been wishful thinking. The Jewish historian Josephus says that he was stricken with a mortal illness, which could well have been some form of cancer. Whether death came instantly or after an illness, the important thing was that with his demise the persecution of the church was at least temporarily halted.

Herod Agrippa II

There's one more Herod — Herod Agrippa II. He was a teenager at the time of his father's death and the Romans did not permit him to succeed immediately to the throne. Military governors were appointed to rule Palestine, until in A.D. 53 Herod Agrippa II was officially given Roman approval to reign over the northern part of Palestine with the title of king. He was the last of the Herodian line and could well have been the best of the lot. He appears in Scripture only in Acts 25 and 26, when he happens to be the guest of the Roman governor Festus and hears Paul defend himself against charges of subversion that had been brought by the Jews. Herod Agrippa II listened to Paul attentively and appreciatively and was the speaker of the famous line, "Almost you persuade me to be a Christian" (King James Version) or "In a short time you think to make me a Christian?" (Revised Standard Version)

The reign of Agrippa and the end of the Herodian line came when there was a rebellion in the land and Jerusalem was destroyed, about A.D. 70.

These are the four Herods who march through the pages of the New Testament:

1) Herod the Great, about 39 B.C. to 2 B.C., who slew the infants at Bethlehem.

2) Herod Antipas, who beheaded John the Baptizer and played a brief role in the trial of Jesus, ruling from 2 B.C. to about A.D. 41.

3) Herod Agrippa I, A.D. 41-44, who persecuted the Christians.

4) Herod Agrippa II, A.D. 53 to about A.D. 70, who chanced to hear Paul's defense and was favorably impressed by it.

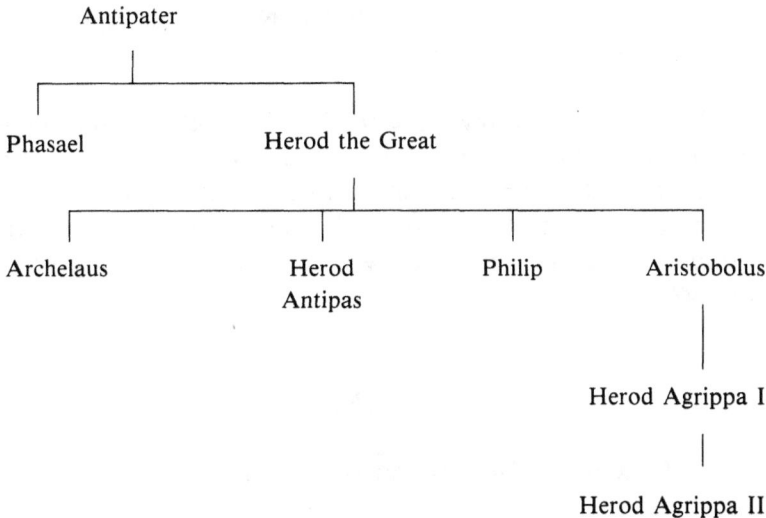

```
                    Antipater
                        |
        ┌───────────────┴───────────────┐
        |                                |
    Phasael                      Herod the Great
                                         |
        ┌──────────────┬─────────────────┬──────────────┐
        |              |                 |              |
    Archelaus        Herod            Philip       Aristobolus
                     Antipas                            |
                                                        |
                                                Herod Agrippa I
                                                        |
                                                        |
                                                Herod Agrippa II
```

Thoughts

(for personal reflection or group discussion)

1. Ruling Israel was a difficult job. Kings were usually chosen by the leaders of the people. The first king was Saul, who had both good and bad points. He was succeeded by David, who was not related to Saul. David and his son Solomon were "good" kings, but after Solomon's death the dynasty broke up in civil war. Is it good for the same family (or party) to stay in power for many generations?

2. When Rome ruled the world, "kings" were really provincial governors. All military power was controlled from Rome. Under this arrangement, there was peace among nations except for occasional rebellions or uprisings. Would such a plan — perhaps with the United Nations in control — produce world peace today?

3. To Rome, the Jews looked like all the other Semitic people. Herod the Great was what we today would call an Arab, but because decisions were made in Rome the Jewish people had to accept him as their ruler. Would outside rule over the Middle East be an acceptable way of compelling peace there today?

Questions

1. How many Herods can you identify?

2. Why did Herod kill the babies in Bethlehem after he learned of the birth of Jesus?

3. Why did Herod build the great temple at Jerusalem?

Chapter 12

From Antioch to the World

Read Acts 13:1-3

About fifteen years after the death and resurrection of Jesus, the most innovative and cosmopolitan Christian congregation was the thriving group at Antioch in Syria. Consisting chiefly of gentile Christians and Jews with a Hellenic background, this lively congregation shows that Jew and gentile could work together in brotherhood and harmony under the banner of Christ. It possessed a world vision that was denied to those in more provincial places. Antioch was where things were made to happen.

The "mother congregation" in Jerusalem still held an important place in the growing Christian movement, but it no longer enjoyed an exclusive right to be the center of authority. While Jerusalem Christians strove to continue their faithful witness despite persecution, other congregations were growing more rapidly in a freer atmosphere. Where Jerusalem resisted change, congregations like Antioch welcomed it.

The Ascendancy of Antioch

One reason for the ascendancy of Antioch was its political and social climate. Originally a Greek colony, it was occupied by Pompey in 64 B.C. and soon afterward became a major military and commercial center. From the Greeks, it inherited an art colony. Its main streets were distinguished by marble colonnades and statues. From the Romans came its university, a good system of roads and water supply. The Romans built great temples, a forum, a theater, baths and other public buildings. From both cultures, Antioch came into a tradition of honest work, careful craftsmanship, dishonest politics and a desire for the luxuries of life.

Favored with a good year-round climate due to its location on the sheltered northeast coast of the Mediterranean, Antioch was a natural commercial hub. Its suburb of Seleucia, sixteen miles away, offered a safe deepwater harbor. It was close to the island of Cyprus and at the point where traders on east-west and north-south routes would cross paths. It was a transfer point for merchandise brought by camel trains from the Orient and then sent by ship to Greece, Rome, Spain and northern Africa.

In this setting, Antioch's church attracted people from all parts of the world, many of them with special education and business experience. They had a sophistication and world-view that was denied to those at Jerusalem and in smaller cities, where a constricted Jewish heritage limited their outlook. The Antiochans were therefore free to be innovators. When they learned of a famine in Judea, they organized a relief effort, setting a pattern for Christian works of selfless mercy that stands to this day. And because they represented a cross-section of ethnic and racial backgrounds, they could visualize the universal appeal of Christ's teaching.

A Congregation With Five Ministers

Like most successful congregations, Antioch's was blessed with excellent leadership. Five "prophets and teachers" comprised their staff of ministers. The five were Barnabas, Symeon who was called Niger (presumably a black man); Lucius of Cyrene; the aristocrat Manaen who had been reared at a royal court, and Saul.

The listing of these five evokes some tempting speculations. Remember that it was Simon of Cyrene who had carried the cross for Jesus. Cyrene was a Greek colony on the north shore of Africa in what today is Libya. It had a large Jewish district. Tradition says that Simon of Cyrene became a convert to Jesus during his burdensome journey on the way of the Cross. Doubtless he would afterward have conversed with some of the disciples and with the women who watched the Crucifixion. He must have told his story over again a thousand times when he got back to his home city. Perhaps he convinced some of the Jews at Cyrene that Jesus was their long-awaited Messiah. At any rate, Lucius of Cyrene could well have been one of those converts who brought their new religion with them when they came to Antioch.

About Manaen we can only conjecture, but his presence as a

leader in the congregation indicates that among these early Christians were people of high birth, social standing and education. Manaen had been raised and educated at the royal court of Herod the Great. We do not know his parentage, but he was a playmate of young Herod Antipas and perhaps his foster brother.

Of Symeon we know nothing, while Barnabas and Saul are familiar figures in this story.

One Sunday while the Antioch congregation was at worship, it received a message which it knew came from the Holy Spirit. "Send out Barnabas and Saul as missionaries to spread God's Word to all nations," the message said. Perhaps this had already been discussed in their midst, but now like the handwriting on the wall at Belshazzar's feast it became clear and urgent. The Antiochans must long have realized that these pastors of theirs had a wider call. They were powerful preachers and leaders, well qualified to plant the Christian faith in other parts of the world and thus to win a growing constituency for their cause.

Barnabas and Saul Head West

So after fasting and praying, the members of the congregation "laid their hands on" Barnabas and Saul and sent them off. The laying on of hands was an ancient blessing indicating that the messengers carried with them the commendation of those who sent them. They sent them off with prayer, for they knew they faced unknown perils. Any travel in those days was a terrible hardship, but travel to and from Antioch was commonplace, since it was a trade center with ships and caravans constantly coming and going.

The command of the Holy Spirit (13:2) placed Barnabas first and Saul second. There is significance in this, for at this time Barnabas was the accepted leader. Although not one of the original Twelve, Barnabas occupied a position of high esteem in the church, both at Jerusalem and Antioch. His generosity and honesty is mentioned (4:36) when he sold a piece of land and brought all the money he received to the church to lay it at the feet of the apostles. He is identified in that instance as a Levite from Cyprus, who was originally named Joseph but was renamed by the apostles. The name Barnabas means "Son of Encouragement" or "Son of Consolation" or "Son of Exhortation." The choice of such a name testifies that the apostles felt that Barnabas had excellent qualities to exhort and encourage others. His activities justified the choice.

When Saul first came to Jerusalem after his conversion and sought admission to the inner circles of the church, only Barnabas gave him the benefit of the doubt and accepted his conversion as genuine. He then prevailed on the others to give Saul a chance to prove himself. In this instance, Barnabas' powers of persuasion and his reconciling spirit were evident.

The confidence which the Christians at Antioch placed in Barnabas is reflected in the commissioning of these first missionaries. They agreed without question that Barnabas should take the lead. Usually we refer to "Paul's first missionary journey," but at the outset the choice for leadership fell on Barnabas, with Saul chosen second. While this arrangement did not last long, it shows the thinking of the "old-line" Christians in Antioch whose reservations in regard to Saul may have been similar to the feelings of the church leaders in Jerusalem.

Barnabas and Saul were not sent out by the other apostles, nor by the Jerusalem congregation with its Judaic background, but by the Antioch Christians with their gentile predominance. It was a step of incalculable importance for the spread of the Gospel and it also proved to be the opportunity for Saul to prove his right to be regarded as a full-fledged participant in the work of the apostles. Up to this time he had been looked upon by many as an upstart, a liability to the church, banished from Jerusalem and kept in second place in Antioch.

With the departure of Barnabas and Saul from Antioch on this missionary journey, the whole outlook for Christianity is being changed. The church is beginning its long movement toward becoming a world religion, not limited by racial or ethnic background or by slavish adherence to the ancient laws of Moses.

Thoughts

(for personal reflection or group discussion)

1. We hear today of a "working class congregation" or a "college congregation." Is it good for a Christian congregation to have members of only one social or economic class? Or should congregations be a cross-section of society? Consider the advantages and disadvantages of each. Where does your congregation fit in?

2. The divine call that sent Barnabas and Saul out to convert the world was evidently originated and supported by the whole Antioch congregation. It was not a mission sought by Barnabas and Saul. In our religious (and political) life, are we better served by self-appointed leaders who campaign for office, or by leaders who must be drafted and may even be reluctant to take the job?

3. The goal of spreading the Gospel to all people came from a predominantly gentile congregation, rather than from Jewish Christians. What does this say about the attitude of both groups?

Questions

1. Where was Antioch?

2. What made the Antioch congregation missionary-minded?

3. Who were the first Christian missionaries? How were they chosen and commissioned?

4. What instructions were given to the missionaries when they were sent out?

5. What dramatic turning-point in Christian history occurred when Barnabas and Saul were sent out?

Chapter 13

Three for the Road

Read Acts 13:4-12

It was actually a trio that set out from Antioch, for John Mark went along to assist the commissioned missionaries Barnabas and Saul. John was a younger man, who had followed Jesus through much of his ministry. Legend may well be mixed with facts in the accounts about Mark, who is best remembered as the writer of one of the Gospels, but by assembling various references we can come up with a lot of information about him.

John Mark's mother Mary owned a house in Jerusalem which was the center of activity for Jesus and his disciples and later for the growing Christian community. Perhaps Mary was a widow. Her husband is never mentioned, but her loyalty to Jesus was shared by her son, an intelligent teenager. He got to know the disciples intimately and frequently accompanied them on trips. He knew Jesus and listened avidly to the words he spoke. Perhaps his mother Mary was related to Barnabas, for (see Colossians 4:10) Mark is referred to as "sister's son to Barnabas" or as "Cousin to Barnabas."

The Naked Runaway

Personal knowledge of the events in the ministry of Jesus is reflected in Mark's Gospel. One revealing incident recorded only by Mark (and for obviously good reasons!) deals with an incident during the capture of Jesus by the soldiers in the Garden of Gethsemane on the night of the Lord's betrayal. (Mark 14:51) It was something only the participant could have known and recorded. It says that a "young man" had followed the disciples into the garden, clad only in a linen cloth or sheet. When the soldiers spotted him and tried to seize him — for whatever reason we do not know — the young man slipped out of the linen cloth and fled away naked.

While we deal only with presumptions in adding to this intriguing incident, it is very likely that the upper room where Jesus ate the last supper with his disciples was in the house of Mary. Mary's teenage son had perhaps been sent to bed early, but with his lively curiosity he would have stayed awake and been an intent listener to the conversation and singing in the upstairs room. When Jesus and the disciples left the house in the middle of the night — an unusual time to be walking the streets of Jerusalem — the young man got up and followed to see what they were going to do. In his hurry he wrapped himself in the most convenient piece of cloth, a bedsheet, since it was customary for people to sleep with no clothes on. Mark pursued the disciples into the garden, where he witnessed the betrayal and seizure of Jesus. Perhaps he ventured a little too close and thus attracted the attention of the soldiers, but when they came after him and caught hold of the sheet he had wrapped about him, he foiled them by nimbly slipping out of the sheet and running away naked, the first "streaker" on record.

The fact that Mark includes this incident in his Gospel tells us something about the loyalty and devotion of the writer, as well as giving an interesting and somewhat humorous sidelight into the events of that night.

Young John Mark was evidently well-liked by the disciples, who welcomed him into their company. In later years we find him accompanying some of them on their journeys. Though he may have been related to Barnabas, he was especially close to Peter, who in his first letter (1 Peter 5:13) calls him "Mark, my son." Clearly this was a spiritual relationship, for other early Christian writers refer to Mark as Peter's "follower" or "interpreter."

When Barnabas and Saul returned to Antioch from Jerusalem after bringing gifts of food and money to the Jerusalem church, John Mark went with them. As we've noted, this was a time of oppression and peril for the Christians at Jerusalem, so perhaps Mark was sent away for his own safety. Like many of the original followers of Jesus, however, Mark had trouble accepting Saul and his aggressive ways. He started out with Barnabas and Saul from Antioch on the missionary trip, but when Saul assumed the leadership of the expedition, John Mark left them and returned to Jerusalem.

Even Church Leaders Squabble

Though we are getting ahead of our story, we must note at this point that Saul was angry about Mark's departure and branded him as a deserter. He expressed derogatory opinions about the young man and was later unwilling to accept him as a traveling companion. This led to sharp words between Barnabas and Saul, with the result that they split up. Mark went off separately with Barnabas, while Paul chose Silas as his traveling companion. (15:36 ff) Mark journeyed with Barnabas and later with Peter, but evidently the rift between him and Saul was eventually healed, because in the second letter to Timothy, written when Saul was an old man, he asks (2 Timothy 4:10) that Mark be brought to him because "he is very useful to me." In his letter to the Colossians and to Philemon, Paul adds greetings from Mark, indicating that Mark had by that time rejoined his circle.

Personal quarrels among Christians are not modern developments! Christians of all periods are human and all the human foibles show up in their character and in their behavior. Even the apostles were in many ways examples of human weakness, avarice and failure. Some wanted preferred positions; Peter denied Jesus; Thomas was cynical; others ran away when danger threatened. They were given strength, a sense of unity and the ability to accomplish extraordinary things only through their mutual faith in Christ. It ought to be gratifying to us, when we regard our own failures and weakness, to realize that God sometimes purposely chose weak, ordinary people and that God understands our human failings. Christians cannot usually claim credit for their accomplishments because of their own ability, but must like Paul attribute their successes to Christ who provides them with strength.

While Mark was still with Barnabas and Saul, they journeyed to the island of Cyprus, situated in the northeast Mediterranean about one hundred miles by sea from Antioch. It was a normal place to start, for it was the native land of Barnabas. There had been followers of Christ on the island at least since the time of Stephen (Acts 11:19), who had visited there and preached to the Jews in the synagogue. Now, some twelve years later, the missionary trio made this their first call. They could get there easily, for there was constant traffic between Antioch's port of Seleucia (also called Pieria) to Salamis on the eastern edge of Cyprus. Cyprus also made a convenient stop for vessels bound from Antioch to Greece or Rome, a place where they could get fresh water and provisions.

The Hazards of First-Century Travel

Since this trip to Cyprus marks the start of a long period of travel by Saul and his companions, as well as by other disciples, a word about travel in biblical times seems in order. Even today we read the advertising slogan, "Getting there is half the fun," but anybody who does much traveling is likely to challenge that assertion. The inconveniences of carrying luggage, standing in line at airports, waiting while planes are delayed, getting caught in traffic jams and finding that accommodations are second-rate or worse when you have paid for first class, are all burdensome. Travel by ship or train has similar disadvantages — lines waiting to get on board, questions about tickets, waiting endlessly for customs clearance, promised taxicabs or rental cars that don't show up. Travel is not always fun, even today when accommodations are supposed to be so comfortable and luxurious.

Consider then how it must have been in Paul's day! Even to get from Antioch to Cyprus must have been a wearying venture. From Antioch city to its seaport was a journey of about sixteen miles. Even on the paved roads which the Romans had built, this could be a four-hour walk. In a wagon or astride a donkey it might take only two hours, but they would be uncomfortable hours. Then came the chore of negotiating with a sea captain for passage on his boat. There were no travel agents, no ticket agencies, no luxury liners, no Queen Elizabeth II and not even a Staten Island ferryboat. Ships were small, with only a small covered portion at the bow or stern. Motive power was provided by oarsmen or by sail if the wind was favorable. To make a trip of one hundred miles took about three days at best, five or six if the weather was bad. The little ships had no cook on board and no dining salon. Passengers carried with them a bag of food, preferably dried fruit or bread that would not spoil. Water supplies were limited. There were no private staterooms. Passengers carried a blanket or pallet and were allowed to bed down on the open deck. It wasn't much fun. Yet Paul, who by this time was a man in his forties, went through constant hardships of this sort on his seemingly endless travels.

Once passage had been arranged, often after much haggling with the captain, there might still be a long wait. There were no established schedules or regular shipping lines. The captain might say, "We leave with the tide tomorrow." But he might also say that the ship would leave only when sufficient cargo and passengers had been assembled to make the trip profitable. That could mean a waiting period of days.

When the travelers reached port, such as the little port of Salamis on Cyprus, they once again had to set out on foot. They could not bring chariots or horses with them, even if they possessed such luxuries. Sometimes they could hire a donkey or even a carriage, but this was unusual. Normally they walked over the dusty and unpaved roads. Between major cities they might traverse some paved Roman roads, for wherever the empire extended its sway it contributed a good road-building program, chiefly to provide quick movement for military material. Such roads were constructed of concrete mixed with stone and bricks, well-drained and often with wells placed at convenient intervals along the roadside so travelers might refresh themselves.

To travel hundreds of miles over such roads was wearisome. Joggers may take delight in getting out at the crack of dawn and covering many miles before breakfast, but for most of us a hundred-mile walk under a hot sun would be a life-threatening experience. Those journeying along the roads therefore took their time, rested frequently and joined together in groups for companionship and conversation, as well as protection. There were inns or khans along major roads, but they were expensive and were rarely used by ordinary travelers. Fortunately, Oriental hospitality helped the wayfarers. They were often received as guests at houses along the way where they could wash and rest and stay safely overnight. The fear of strangers that compels us to put locks and chains on doors had not at that time destroyed the spirit of helpfulness which welcomed visitors who might bring news or interesting conversation.

Fortunately for Saul, there were also people who were friendly toward the new Christian teachings and who opened their homes to him so that they might have the chance to learn about the Gospel he preached.

Good News for Cyprus

After landing at Salamis, Barnabas, Saul and Mark journeyed the whole length of the island, about one hundred miles. They probably went along a Roman road built on the south side of the island until they reached the port city of Paphos at the western end. They preached and taught as they went, so by the time they got to Paphos word about their message had preceded them and evidently had become an important topic of conversation. As a result, an interesting encounter took place. Sergius Paulus, the Roman proconsul or governor of the province of Cyprus, summoned Barnabas and Saul and asked to hear the message from God which they proclaimed.

Sergius Paulus, whose historicity is verified by inscriptions on tablets found on Cyprus, was a man of high standing with much power. In the Roman scheme, a proconsul ranked somewhat higher than a procurator. Pontius Pilate was procurator of Judea, so Sergius Paulus was an official of higher rank than Pilate. This proconsul took the initiative in calling the missionaries to him and listened carefully to what they had to say. Described as a "man of intelligence," the proconsul recognized the growing importance of this new religion and took the opportunity to learn more about it. As a Roman official, he could never publicly embrace Christianity, but as a man of learning and intellectual curiosity he studied its teachings and evidently recognized their superiority over the superstitious religions which prevailed in the land.

Magician in the Dark

The willingness of the proconsul to give a favorable audience to the Christians stirred opposition from the leaders of the island's superstitious sects. Barnabas and Saul were promptly challenged by a man named Bar-Jesus or Elymas, described as a Jew who claimed to be a prophet and who had skill in working magic. Saul, as usual, answered the challenge aggressively. Either testing his power or completely sure of himself, Saul denounced the magician and invoked a curse of temporary blindness on him. Saul's imprecation worked. Elymas was enveloped by "mist and darkness" and had to ask people to lead him around like a blind man. The proconsul was "astonished," which may be putting it mildly! But he believed, although this work of magic by Saul strangely resembles the very kind of superstitious religion which Elymas also represented.

In the magician's blindness there is a sort of parallel to Saul's own experience. Saul had been spiritually blind and was then actually physically blind for a few days before he saw the light both literally and figuratively and recognized the lordship of Jesus Christ. Now the same sort of thing is happening to this "prophet" on Cyprus. Whether this was hysterical blindness or something similar, we don't know. Elymas suffered blindness only "for a time," so he later regained his vision. Whether or not he embraced the Christian faith remains a mystery.

The "miracle" of striking Elymas blind and thus persuading the proconsul to believe is only incidental to something else that took place, however. The most important thing in this little story is that *Saul* now steps forward to take the leadership away from Barnabas and that he is hereafter referred to as *Paul*, his gentile name. Hitherto he has been Saul, a Jew from Tarsus who by a miraculous conversion became a follower of Christ. Now he is Paul, a Roman citizen and a champion of the faith, an opponent of all that is false and superstitious. As a Roman, he had privilege and standing in the Roman world which his Jewish name would have concealed.

Along with the change in name, there is another change. The order of precedence is from this point on reversed. Whereas the church at Antioch sent out "Barnabas and Saul," we read hereafter of "Paul and his company" or "Paul and Barnabas." For weal or woe, Paul is now in the driver's seat.

When Paul and Barnabas had completed their affairs at Paphos, they made a sea voyage to Pamphylia (on Turkey's southern coast), disembarking at the seaport village of Attalia. The place survives to this day as a commercial port, now named Antalya. Then they proceeded a few miles north to the city of Perga.

On to Perga

The record simply says "They set sail from Paphos and came to Perga in Pamphylia." That sounds as easy as getting in your car for a drive. Actually, it was an ordeal. The voyage meant days or weeks of discomfort, miserable shipboard food, tainted water, lack of sanitary facilities and sleeping on the hard deck of a boat, perhaps in pelting rain or fog or storm. The entire trip made by Paul and Barnabas from Antioch in Syria through Cyprus and Asia Minor and back covered about 1,200 miles. Today we would make a trip of such length in three hours by airplane or in less than three days by automobile, if roads were available. It took Paul and his companions three years! Of course, there were delays along the way. They paused in various communities long enough to preach the Gospel and to establish small groups of believers into units that later became flourishing congregations. They encountered setbacks from hostile Jews, from nature and from their own frailty.

The effects of the grueling travel became evident at Perga. First, John Mark left them and returned to Jerusalem, arousing Paul's anger. There is no hint of the reason for Mark's sudden withdrawal. Maybe other people had joined the entourage, for the narrative says that "Paul and his company" made the crossing from Paphos to Perga. Mark may have felt that he was no longer needed. Maybe Mark was homesick, for never before had he been so far away from Jerusalem. Possibly he felt that the trip into Pamphylia exceeded the terms of the commission given to Paul. Maybe there was a ship leaving for Antioch or Caesarea, offering a homebound opportunity that might not occur again. A later mention of the situation says that Mark "deserted," which implies dissatisfaction or unhappiness on his part.

Another question is raised by the immediate departure of Paul and Barnabas from Perga for the inland city of Antioch in Pisidia. Both Attalia and Perga were large and open cities, certainly with some Jewish inhabitants. It would have been more natural for the missionaries to have stayed at least for a short time, to rest up and to preach. But there's also a possibility that Paul was seriously ill at this time and that Mark regarded further travel as foolhardy. Whatever it was, some conflict arose when the group reached Perga, leading to Mark's defection and to the immediate getaway of Paul and Barnabas for the mountain country.

Thoughts

(for personal reflection or group discussion)

1. The friction between Barnabas and Saul and Mark is not fully explained. Was Mark just homesick, or did his gentle personality clash with Saul's abrasiveness? Are there counterparts for these three in your congregation? How can Christians of differing temperaments get along?

2. What do you make of Saul's first "miracle"? Even if the magician Bar-Jesus was a nuisance and a pest, was Saul's action justified?

3. In our day, people sometimes change their names in order to shed some past deficiency. What meanings can be found in the missionary's transition from Saul to Paul?

Questions

1. What three persons started out on the first missionary journey?

2. What was Mark's relation to Saul? How did they get along?

3. Why is Saul now referred to as Paul?

4. What means of travel were used by the missionaries?

5. What changes occurred when the missionaries reached Perga?

Chapter 14

Forward into Galatia

Read Acts 13:13-52

Biblical names can confuse casual readers. Even serious Bible scholars have their troubles with some of them. Most of us can identify Jerusalem and Bethlehem and even Capernaum, but we get a little lost when we hear about Paphos and Perga, Pamphylia and Pisidia all in one breath!

Another Antioch

When Paul left Perga with "his company" he traveled northward to the small city of Antioch in (or near) Pisidia. The identification as "in Pisidia" is necessary to differentiate this Antioch from the larger Antioch in Syria, where the expedition had originated. There had been five Syrian kings named Antiochas, and many cities and towns bore their name.

Antioch in Pisidia is on the Plateau of Anatolia, which today comprises central Turkey. At Paul's time it was under Roman rule, but was still a center of Greek influence and culture. Its modern counterpart is Aksehir, a city of about 25,000 people.

In this area Paul also visited Lystra, Iconium and Derbe. When he later wrote his epistle to the Galatians, he addressed it to all four churches in this area — Antioch in Pisidia, Iconium, Lystra and Derbe. Rather than trying to use the tongue-twisting names of cities and provinces, it is easier to do as Paul did and combine the whole region under the name of Galatia. The people in these four cities were the ones who have been given a sort of immortality because they were the recipients of Paul's great little letter on Christian liberty which we know as the Epistle to the Galatians.

"They passed on from Perga and came to Antioch in Pisidia." This is the concise way in which Luke describes the journey, but it leaves us strangely unsatisfied. Though it was a journey of only about one hundred miles, the description of the trip — or rather the lack of description — is deceptive.

To travel 100 miles on foot over mountainous country would be a tiring journey, at best. However, Paul and his companions made this trip over rough and rarely-used mountain trails, crossing Turkey's most rugged mountain range, the Taurus mountains. Several peaks are more than two miles high and are always snowcapped. There were then five passes through the mountains from the seacoast to the interior plateau, called the Cilician Gates. The difficulty of passage through these passes caused the range to be considered an impenetrable barrier to commercial travel or to military invasion of interior Turkey. There were also two large rivers which Paul's entourage had to ford, for there were no bridges. At times during the year, melting snow turned the rivers into raging torrents which engulfed anybody foolish enough to try to cross them. Sometimes a rope was stretched from one side to the other for travelers to cling to and thus help to keep their footing.

This arduous journey is reported only in a few brief words. When we read it, it sounds as easy as walking down the street. While the writer of Acts surely does not want to mislead us, in this case the brevity of the account seriously understates the facts.

Because the Book of Acts is self-contained and not paralleled by other biblical accounts, it's difficult to check for corroborative detail which might explain more than the bare text. In the account of the life and work of Jesus, we have four Gospels which supplement and authenticate one another. The search for supportive evidence in Acts requires a little more work.

What Was Ailing Paul?

When we turn to Paul's letter to the Galatians, we learn something more about this journey. In Galatians 4:12-15, Paul refers to his arrival at Antioch, saying, "You know that it was because of a bodily ailment that I preached the Gospel to you at first; and though my condition was a trial to you, you did not scorn or despise me . . . For I bear you witness, that, if possible, you would have plucked out your eyes and given them to me."

Paul's testimony thus indicates that a bodily ailment afflicted him when he came to Antioch, adding to the burdens and danger of that trip over the mountains. The seriousness of his condition is indicated by the fact that he was a "trial" to those people — a sick stranger who needed special attention. He must have been deathly sick. What the sickness was, we do not know, but the reference to the fact that their generosity and concern were such that they would have given Paul their own eyes, if possible, rouses the supposition that it was eye trouble. Was it a recurrence of the blindness that had stricken him on the Damascus Road? Or was it possibly snow blindness from some harrowing experience as he crossed the high mountains? Or was it something that had affected him earlier and had caused his hasty departure from Perga?

Paul's epistles imply that he suffered from eye trouble, since others usually wrote the message for him and he added a personal greeting at the end of the letter in his own hand. If he wrote the letter to the Galatians himself, for instance, he must have done it in unusually large script, for at the close he remarks about "what large letters I am writing to you with my own hand."

Another conjecture includes the idea that Paul was epileptic, which would help account for his occasional seizures, but here no supporting evidence is found. Some hold to the theory that Paul contracted malaria, a prevalent disease in the low country along the shore of Turkey. This would have left him weakened and feverish and would help account for his swift departure from the seacoast to the higher altitudes of the interior.

Whatever was actually the case, we are indebted to Paul's own comment in his letter to the Galatians for shedding some light on the harshness of this journey, which in Luke's words is made to sound like an easy overnight trip.

Paul, Popular Preacher

Though Paul arrived at Antioch in a state of ill health, the Jewish community there was evidently extremely gracious and hospitable. They nursed the sick traveler and cared for him. As soon as Paul had recovered, he attended the synagogue and was extended the courtesy often given to Jews from other communities, to speak a word of greeting and encouragement.

Paul's presentation followed a familiar pattern, which seems to

mark the preaching of all the disciples to Jewish audiences throughout this period. He described the power of God in the life of the
people of Israel, pointing out the mighty works that God did in the
time of Moses and through the lives of the prophets. Then he explained that the promises made through the voice of the prophets
foretold the coming of a Savior or Messiah, who would bring healing and redemption to his people. These promises, the sermon continued, were fulfilled in the life and work of Jesus, who by his atoning
death on the cross brought freedom from the law and the promise
of eternal life.

Such a sermon relied on the hearers' knowledge of the history
of Israel. It invoked names like Moses, Samuel, Saul, David and
Abraham — great heroes of faith who were revered by Jews
everywhere.

Simple as it was, this message and its format provided the essen-
tial truths required in those days. The Gospels had not yet been written. Even if they had, few of these hearers would have been
acquainted with them. The plain narrative of redemption according
to God's plan was therefore exciting and new to the audiences. They
pleaded to hear it over and over again, just as children beg to have
a familiar story repeated.

When Paul had finished his sermon, the people therefore asked
him to come back the next sabbath to repeat the message. They evidently also besieged Paul and Barnabas with questions and comments. Surely they would have expressed concerns about the future
of Judaism now that a new revelation had come, about the need for
continuing in the law, about the methods by which they might embrace in their own lives the freedom which Paul announced. Not
wishing to precipitate a controversy which would erupt into a scene
of dissension in the synagogue, Paul and Barnabas simply urged them
to be patient and to "continue in the grace of God."

The news of Paul's preaching must have spread like wildfire
through the small city. The message was repeated not only among
the Jewish community but in gentile circles as well. Even allowing
for some hyperbole by the reporter, the effect was striking. The following sabbath "almost the whole city gathered together" to listen
to the apostles. There were "multitudes" present. It must have been
an event that shook up the whole town.

When Success Turns Sour

The very success of the visiting preachers turned some of the orthodox Jewish leaders against Paul and Barnabas. They resented the fact that the promise which they had considered theirs alone was now to be shared with outsiders. They clung to their clannish conviction that the Jews were God's chosen people and that by opening the floodgates to everybody the missionaries were violating the tradition of Jewish exclusiveness.

This jealous or self-centered reaction was repeated in other places. With the expansion of the Christian message to embrace the gentiles as well as the Jews, the Jews — or at least some of them — felt compromised and cheated. They were in their own eyes a chosen and unique people. It was this conviction that had enabled them to endure oppression and vilification throughout the centuries and to retain an arrogant attitude toward the non-Jews. To be told now that they must share their ancient faith with gentiles whom they considered inferior was a bitter blow. They reacted by striking back at the messengers who brought news of the new revelation in Jesus.

When some of the Jewish leaders reviled and chastised Paul and Barnabas for permitting gentiles to hear their message, the apostles rebuked them for their narrowness and bigotry. "You are indeed the people chosen by God to bring forth his redeeming grace for the whole world," Paul said. "You are the ones ordained by God to hear his word. But since you thrust it from you, and evidently judge yourselves unworthy of eternal life, we turn to the gentiles, for this is what God has commanded."

Naturally, the gentiles were delighted. They glorified the word of God and "as many as were ordained to eternal life believed." The latter statement seems to imply some kind of predestination, as though God had in advance selected a certain number of gentiles to be granted the fruits of faith in Christ. Often theological arguments can be based on a small phrase like this, which suggests a denial of free choice. It is true that Paul's teaching had some implications of predestination. Paul subscribed to the doctrine that God has a purpose in everything he does. He would not therefore have manifested his glory through the coming of Jesus into the world unless there were individuals ready to accept him. In this sense, God preordained some individuals to be saved. However, Paul's teaching does not in any way negate the doctrine of the freedom of the

118

will, which permits each individual to respond to God's Word either by joyfully accepting it or by hardening his heart and turning a deaf ear to it.

When people heard the words of salvation and hardened their hearts against it, they could be said to have rejected and disobeyed the heavenly vision that was revealed to them. Paul himself in his early life fell into this category. He knew much about Jesus, but refused to accept him. Later, when the time for his conversion came, he could state proudly that he "was not disobedient to the heavenly vision." The Jewish conception of predestination, which regarded the Jewish nation as the sole segment of humankind that was to be the channel for God's grace, was never a part of Paul's preaching.

"We turn to the gentiles, for so the Lord has commanded," Paul admonished the jealous Jews of Antioch. This led to a division of the sort which plagued the whole church during these early decades. There were three obstinate groups: the Jews who refused to accept the Word of God as revealed in Jesus, the Jews who accepted it only as a special revelation for Jews, and the receptive Jews and gentiles who saw the universal meaning of God's revelation as a bringer of light and hope and salvation to people everywhere.

A better rendering of the phrase about being "ordained" to eternal life would be, "As many as were open to the teaching about eternal life believed." No one was barred from believing. On the other hand, no special mark of grace was placed by God upon particular individuals to compel them to accept the promises that Paul proclaimed.

The Jewish Counter-Attack

The achievement of the disciples in winning a large number of Jews and gentiles to the way of life which they advocated had its usual counter-effect. Jews who resisted and rejected their preaching plotted against them, creating open antagonism between the synagogue and the new group of believers. Somehow the Jews persuaded "devout women of high standing and the leading men of the city" to stir up opposition to Paul and Barnabas. They created disorder in the streets and potential riots of some sort. By doing so they expected to persuade the Roman magistrates to expel the preachers as disturbers of the peace. Roman rule was tolerant of all established religions, but extremely wary of new ones that might somehow undermine the government. Judaism was therefore permitted throughout the Roman Empire, since it was a close-knit group which kept to itself in its ghetto and confined its religious activities to the home and the synagogue. Jews as a rule did no street preaching or proselyting, made no effort to teach or convert non-Jews, and asked only to be left alone.

Paul tried to get similar protection for his followers by proclaiming it as true Judaism and the Christian church as the true Israel. He makes this point later in his letter to these same Galatians. However, local Roman magistrates would probably not be interested in listening to theological arguments, nor would they have the ability to judge who was a true Jew and who was not. If there was any likelihood of a civil disorder because of this new teaching, the missionary preachers would be ousted from the city without delay.

Aware of this, Paul and Barnabas shook the dust of Antioch from their feet and departed. In his letter to Timothy (2 Timothy 3:11) Paul remarks on the sufferings and persecutions which he endured at Antioch, Iconium and Lystra, but without giving further detail. All we know is that the roof caved in on this first missionary effort at Antioch in Pisidia and the apostles left hurriedly. While they at that time established no continuing Christian congregation in Antioch because of their hasty departure, they left behind a city which had been stirred by hearing the message of the Gospel and a nucleus of people who were ready to confess their faith in Jesus. About one year later, Paul and Barnabas again visited Antioch (14:21) and quietly encouraged the Christians there to continue in their faith. They then appointed elders to establish more firmly the worship and work that had been started.

Thoughts

(for personal reflection or group discussion)

1. In Paul's writings, he often refers to bodily ailments, yet he plodded along disregarding his health and allowing little or no time for rest and recreation. Is this good stewardship of one's physical strength? Just how much does God expect of us?

2. Paul often preached to people who had never heard of Jesus. Put yourself in the same situation. What would you say to someone?

3. If God knows what we are going to do before we make up our own minds, what good is freedom of choice? If we make the wrong decisions, can we blame God for not stopping us? Think about the doctrine of predestination and its place (if any) in Christian theology.

Questions

1. To whom did Paul write the *Epistle to the Galatians*? Where or what is Galatia?

2. How was Paul's condition when he got to Antioch in Pisidia?

3. What divisions developed in the synagogue after Paul's preaching?

4. How did Paul make out in his first effort to establish a Christian congregation?

5. Is it realistic to hope that everything we attempt for God will bring some good result?

Chapter 15

Another god for Lystra

Read Acts 14:1-28

The hasty exit from Antioch evidently did not dampen the spirit of Paul's group. Filled with joy and enthusiasm, they trudged eastward on the next leg of their journey. The area in which they were traveling was not very far from Paul's native city of Tarsus and he may have walked the same road before. He evidently knew the countryside well and had planned a route that would take him to three or four of the small cities on the plain. The chief reason the missionary trip took this eastward direction must have been Paul's acquaintance with the area and its people. There were bigger cities toward the west which would have greeted the missionaries with equal fervor and offered richer opportunities.

Ministry in Iconium

They first came to Iconium, which lies about 90 miles east of Antioch on the Plateau of Anatolia. Iconium thrives today as the modern city of Konya with nearly 250,000 population. It lies on a high fertile plain noted for its agricultural products and the raising of livestock, but it's now a manufacturing center. In Paul's day it was a prospering market town. Its Jewish community was smaller than the one at Antioch and there were fewer Greeks, most of the population consisting of native Anatolians.

At Iconium the pattern that had been established at Antioch repeated itself. Paul and Barnabas preached in the synagogue and won many followers among both Jews and Greeks. The few Romans in the area, one must remember, were mostly soldiers or government officials who were pledged to a belief in the deity of their emperor, so they were not too likely to jump on a Christian bandwagon.

Once the popularity of Paul and Barnabas reached the point where the leaders of the Jewish synagogue felt threatened, they "stirred up the gentiles and poisoned their minds." In spite of this, Paul and Barnabas remained at Iconium for a "long time," until the division in the city broke out into open hostility. The Jewish community itself was divided, with some accepting the message brought by the missionaries while others vehemently opposed it. The Greek community was similarly divided. The native population, lacking the Judaic background which explained the coming of a messiah or the philosophic bent which characterized Greek thought, must have been somewhat indifferent to the whole affair.

Timothy's Home Town

Fearing bodily harm, Paul and his company ended their stay at Iconium and went to Lystra (modern Hatun-Serai, about 25 miles south of Konya) and to Derbe. The terms used by the reporter who wrote Acts seem to indicate that they shuttled back and forth between Lystra and Derbe and that they also took the Gospel into the surrounding country, perhaps preaching in other small communities. At Derbe, Paul would have been only fifty miles away from his home town of Tarsus, but a rugged range of 7,000-foot mountains barred the way.

Lystra is important for two reasons. It gives us one of the most delightful humorous incidents in all of Paul's travels; and it is the home city of Timothy, who later became Paul's companion and a leader in the church.

Lystra was a stronghold for the pagan religion of the Greeks. There were some Jews there, for Timothy's mother Eunice was Jewish but had married a gentile, which would seem to indicate that the Jews of Lystra were not strict adherents to the law. There is no mention of a synagogue either at Lystra or Derbe.

To understand the religious situation at Lystra, some information about the religion of the Greeks is helpful. The Greeks believed in a whole pantheon of gods and goddesses, each of whom looked after certain needs. There was a goddess of dawn, to make sure the sun rose. There was a goddess of the harvest. Chief of their gods was Zeus, whose great weapon was a thunderbolt. Zeus had many wives among the goddesses and one of his sons was Hermes, who was the god ruling matters of fertility, travelers, youth — and who also served as a messenger of the gods. All these gods and goddesses had human characteristics and appearance (anthropomorphism) and they also had human frailties. For instance, one of them sprained his ankle and limped for a while. This isn't what you normally expect of gods, but the Greeks felt more kindly toward gods who could share human pain and human joy. Their gods even cheated one another and sometimes played jokes on one another. Once in a while they took special interest in some event taking place among mortals and came down to earth.

In Lystra there was a tradition that once upon a time the great Zeus had come down along with his son Hermes and paid a visit to two peasants in the town. Because of this great favor from the supreme god, the town felt richly blessed and the people built a great temple in front of the city dedicated to Zeus. An inscription has been found near Lystra to "Zeus before the city," referring to this temple. In the easygoing pattern of Greek religion, it was deemed quite possible that at any time a god or goddess might come down and be seen among the people.

As a result, a very unusual thing happened when Paul and Barnabas came into the city. A man who had been a cripple from birth was sitting at the roadside. His feet were useless and he had never been able to walk. This man's attention was directed at Paul, for when Paul came into such a city he evidently talked to everybody in sight. It may not be irreverent to classify Paul as a sort of super-salesman. He walked along city streets buttonholing people and telling them the Good News about Jesus. It got him into trouble sometimes, but it also attracted attention, which was what Paul had in mind. Paul never stopped talking. "We are here to tell you about Jesus of Nazareth, whom God has sent to be a Savior for all people," Paul would say to some complete stranger. Some hearers would brush him aside, others would regard him as slightly queer, but quite a few would be impressed by what he was saying and by the sincerity of his convictions.

The cripple at Lystra paid close attention to Paul's words. He may not have had much choice, because Paul kept talking all the time and the helpless man could not move away. But Paul observed him intently and realized that hope was stirring within the crippled man's heart. Maybe this great Savior whom Paul proclaimed could make him well!

One can only wonder what went through Paul's mind. Perhaps he recalled what had happened in the earliest days of the church, when Peter and John encountered a similar situation at the Gate Beautiful of the temple at Jerusalem. Paul must have pondered that miracle many times. It was not the power of Peter that made it happen, but the power of faith in God through Christ which flowed through Peter. If it had happened in Jerusalem, why not in Lystra? So Paul cried in a loud voice, "Stand upright on your feet!" The power of faith triumphed once more, for the crippled man sprang up and walked.

Two Cases of Mistaken Identity

Paul's loud command must have attracted attention. By this time, a sizeable crowd had drawn around him. When the people saw what he had done, they reacted as one might expect. They did not know who Paul was, but they saw what he did and exclaimed, "The gods are here again! They have come down to us in the likeness of men!" After all, who else could perform a miracle?

Word spread rapidly through the town that Zeus and Hermes had returned. Barnabas they called Zeus, the greater god, and Paul they acclaimed as Hermes. If that seems odd, remember that Paul did all the talking. In the eyes of the people, the greater god would remain silent and aloof while the lesser one did the chores. Barnabas was therefore accredited as the superior god because he talked less and did less! Probably Barnabas was also taller and stronger than Paul, who was small in stature.

Interestingly, the people spoke in Lycaonian, a dialect which Paul and Barnabas may not have understood. In any event, things got swiftly out of hand. Great elation was aroused among the people and they poured into the streets to hold a special ceremony in honor of what they considered to be divine visitors. The priest of the temple was summoned and he brought oxen and garlands to the gates to offer sacrifice to the two supposed gods. This was a major sacrifice, for oxen are large animals and offering up two oxen meant that this was considered a momentous event.

Paul and Barnabas at that moment could have had anything they wanted from the people, but instead they were getting exactly what they did not want. They were getting personal adulation from the crowd and were strengthening the people in their pagan beliefs. Amid

all the shouting and confusion, it was difficult for them to get a moment of quiet to persuade the people that they were on the wrong
track. Paul may have felt that he was better off when he was being
vilified and condemned than when he was being idolized.

To stop the ceremony, Paul and Barnabas rushed into the midst
of the crowd, shouting and waving for attention and tearing their
garments. To tear one's garment was a sign of extreme emotion or
agony and it had sufficient effect to permit Paul to make himself
heard.

The missionaries then made a short speech, perhaps repeating
it over and over. "Men, why are you doing this? We are only human beings like you. We represent a living God, who even though
you do not know him has not left himself without witness among
you, for he has given you the rain and the fruitful seasons and has
filled your stomachs with food and your hearts with gladness."

The speech was typical of Paul's approach to uneducated pagans.
There was no way of reaching such people by telling them about
Jewish prophets and their hope for a Messiah, for these people knew
nothing about Judaism and would not have understood the message.
Paul therefore spoke about the god of nature, the "unknown" liv-
ing God who provides everything to satisfy the needs of humankind.
It was a proper reference, because God is the god of nature as well
as of everything else.

From Praise to Persecution

The acclamation did not last long. We go from the heights to
the depths. Typical of the fickleness of a crowd that can shout
"Hosanna!" one day and "Crucify him!" a few days later, the people at Lystra turned against Paul and Barnabas. Perhaps they felt
somewhat chagrined to find that these were not really gods. People
don't like to be made to appear foolish.

Then Jews from Antioch and Iconium came to the city and informed the local people that Paul and Barnabas had been driven
out of their communities. This news inflamed the Lystrans to such
a degree that they actually committed an act of violence, stoning
Paul and dragging him out of the city. Others in the group were evidently unhurt, for they gathered around Paul, helped him to his feet
and brought him back into the city. On the next morning Paul and
Barnabas left Lystra and went to Derbe, where they were able to

preach the Gospel freely and to make many disciples.

The Lystra incident was not without some success. When Paul came back to the city a few years later on his second missionary journey, he found among the disciples there a young man named Timothy. Timothy was the son of a Jewish woman who had accepted the Christian faith, but his father was a Greek and presumably pagan. Although no mention of Timothy or his parents occurs in the account of this first visit to Lystra, it is reasonable to assume that Timothy's introduction to Christianity came at this time.

A Good Visit to Derbe

After the debacle at Lystra, the visit to Derbe must have been profitable and reassuring. Jewish persecutors did not follow the disciples, so they were able to preach without hindrance. With no synagogue at Derbe, their hearers must have been recruited from the gentiles. There may, however, have been a few Jews in the city who kept up some of their religious observances. Because of the strong family ties among Jews of all generations, the home has been the place for the instilling and nurture of the faith to a greater degree than the school or synagogue. Paul and Barnabas in some way succeeded in gathering a congregation and appointing elders to lead it in worship and in the cultivation of the faith.

From Derbe, it would have been logical for Paul and his company to cross the mountains to Tarsus and return to Antioch in Syria by this shorter route. They chose, however, to retrace their steps westward, revisiting the cities of Lystra, Iconium and Antioch in Pisidia with their bittersweet memories. The second visit gave them a chance to stabilize and encourage the Christian communities which they had been forced to abandon in so great a hurry.

In each place they exhorted the people to remain faithful, pointing out, perhaps from their personal experience, that the entrance to the kingdom of God is often beset by tribulations. In each place they also appointed elders to continue the worship and witness and keep the faith alive. Keep it alive they did, as we know from Paul's later visits and letters. The return visits were unmarked by violence or opposition, perhaps because the missionaries confined their work to strengthening the faith of those already committed. If they did any street preaching or public haranguing, it is not reported. Most people therefore did not know that the disciples were back in town.

In the volatile street life of the Oriental cities, small riots are quickly forgotten. Since this return visit took place at least a year after the first visit, the missionaries could doubtless move unnoticed through the streets.

Once again they made the difficult trip from Antioch in Pisida to the coastal cities of Perga and Attalia, but this time Paul was in better health and spirits. It was also easier to descend from the mountains in the interior to the lower lands along the coast than it had been to climb the other way. At Perga, the city through which they had passed silently and hurriedly, they paused long enough to do some preaching and teaching. Then from the port of Attalia they took a ship which bore them back directly to Antioch in Syria, sailing past the island of Cyprus. It sounds so easy! But it had been a three-year trip, encompassing sickness, hardship, rejection, and, in Paul's case, being stoned and left for dead. Nevertheless they came back with great joy, for they could report to the Antioch church that Christian outposts had been established on Cyprus and in at least three cities of Galatia. The Gospel had been well-received by the gentiles and God had opened a door of faith for them. The major problems on the trip, besides health, had stemmed from opposition by some of the Jews, whose self-righteous claim to exclusive possession of the promises of God led to hatred and violence. No wonder Paul later wrote that the Christian church is the true Israel, the Israel after the spirit, while the old Israel has judged itself unworthy of eternal life.

Thoughts

(for personal reflection or group discussion)

1. In Galatia, people worshiped many different gods. Looking on the religious scene in our communities today, how are we different?

2. Greek gods shared human pain and joy. Consider how this relates to the humanity of Jesus. Would our feelings toward Jesus be different if he was totally unlike us, the "absolute other" of Kirkegaard's teaching?

3. There are times when the personality of the preacher may get in the way of the message. Good preachers know this and avoid it. Luther, for example, wanted his followers called "evangelicals" rather than "Lutherans." Do some religious leaders of our day cloud the Gospel message?

Questions

1. When did Paul first meet Timothy?

2. What god or gods did the Greeks worship? How did their religion differ from that of the Jews?

3. Name the chief god of the Greeks.

4. What part does the faith of an individual play in any miracle? Can a miracle occur without faith?

5. Who did the people of Lystra think Paul and Barnabas were?

6. How did the events at Lystra compare with those in Jerusalem during Holy Week?

Postscript to *Journey Through Acts*, Part One

We have now followed the adventures of the apostles during the early days of the Christian era and have also traveled for three years with Paul on his first missionary journey. We have witnessed the development of the Followers of the Way from a few trembling disciples huddled in an upper room in Jerusalem to a movement with congregations or communities in cities and towns throughout the Roman world. No longer is the survival of the Gospel of Jesus Christ dependent on any single group or congregation, for the message of salvation is now believed and preached in dozens, perhaps hundreds, of places.

But this is merely the beginning. Much more is to happen before the first generation of friends and followers of Jesus passes away.

For technical production reasons, our story is printed in two volumes. It continues in Part Two, *Journey Through Acts, The Road to Rome.*

About the Author

The Rev. Albert P. Stauderman, D.D., Litt.D., is a Lutheran clergyman, author and journalist. For twenty-seven years he was associated with *The Lutheran*, national news magazine of the Evangelical Lutheran Church in America, as associate editor, editor and director of publication. He retired in 1978 and resides on Singer Island, Florida.

Born in Mount Vernon, New York, Dr. Stauderman was graduated in 1931 from Wagner College, Staten Island, New York. He pursued graduate study at Columbia University and Hartwick Lutheran Theological Seminary. He holds degrees from Wagner and Hartwick and received honorary doctorates from Wagner and from Susquehanna University.

Before entering the ordained ministry, he was for six years a reporter and copy editor for the *New York Times*. From 1935-51 he was pastor of St. Paul's Lutheran Church, Teaneck, New Jersey, which grew during his pastorate to be the largest Lutheran congregation in the state. He was one of the organizers of the Lutheran Synod of New Jersey and served on many national boards and committees of the church. He was president of the National Lutheran Editors Association and a director of the Associated Church Press. In 1965 he received the Distinguished Service Award from Lutheran Brotherhood.

Dr. Stauderman went to Philadelphia in 1951 as associate editor of *The Lutheran* and managing editor of the Muhlenberg Press. He was editor and publisher of the magazine from 1970 until his retirement. He is author of many magazine articles and eleven books, including *Facts About Lutherans*, *Earth Has No Sorrow*, *Forty Proven Ways to a Successful Church*, *Let Me Illustrate*, and *Five Prophets for Today*.

Since his retirement, he has served as interim pastor for congregations in Boca Raton, Tequesta and Lake Park, Florida, and has continued writing and leading seminars and Bible study groups.